MORAL WISDOM
IN THE ALLOCATION
OF ECONOMIC RESOURCES

Paul C. Goelz

Editor

St. Mary's University Press
San Antonio, Texas

THE ST. MARY'S UNIVERSITY SERIES

An Economic Philosophy for a Free People

Economic Freedom in the Eighties

Ireland: Freeing the Free Enterprise System

The Economic System of Free Enterprise:
Its Judeo-Christian Values
And Philosophical Concepts

MORAL WISDOM
IN THE ALLOCATION
OF ECONOMIC RESOURCES

Proceedings of the Fifth
National Symposium on the
Philosophy of Free Enterprise

Conducted by

St. Mary's University of San Antonio

1986-87

Paul C. Goelz
Editor

St. Mary's University Press
San Antonio, Texas

Library of Congress 88-60510
ISBN 0-945632-00-2
Printed by Best Printing Co., Austin, Texas
Bound by Custom Bookbinders, Austin, Texas
Printed in the United States of America

Dedication

This volume is dedicated to the generations of students, faculty, and staff of our School of Business and Administration, and their friends in the Business profession, who have contributed so much to the advancement of learning at St. Mary's University – and to Albert and Margaret Alkek who through their substantial assistance assure still greater academic excellence.

CONTENTS

Preface

Professional education for Business and Administration has advanced significantly during the past seventy-five years. However, attention has not been focused sufficiently on those Judeo-Christian values and philosophical concepts which are the soul of the Market System of Economics.

In the School of Business and Administration of St. Mary's University for more than a decade our Symposia have brought to our campus national and international leaders in thought and action. The purpose is to formulate and articulate that ethos which should constitute moral wisdom for the allocation of economic resources.

Professor Erik von Kuehnelt-Leddihn of Austria in his perspective keynote of this Symposium, which these Proceedings record, admonishes:

> Free Enterprise fosters inequalities and there is an egalitarian temptation in all of Christianity, but we are all unequal in every respect and, above all, in the eyes of God. If Judas Iscariot were equal to John the Baptist, Christianity could close shop. Some theologians play tricks by arguing adverbially that we equally have bodies, equally have souls, and equally are called for salvation, but I and the Rockefellers equally have banking accounts although not equal banking accounts. *Eleutheria*, freedom, is mentioned in the Bible again and again, but not *isotes* in the sense of equality, but only of equity. Not equality is justice, but Ulpian's *suum cuique* "to everybody his due." Still, the Trojan asses of the theological demi-monde clamoring for the consensus of the masses want it differently. They apparently ache for the Provider State. Yet, Pius XII warned them already way back in 1952 and spoke about "the protection of the individual and the family from an all-embracing socialization, a process in whose terminal stage the terrifying vision of the Leviathan State would become a gruesome reality. The Church is going to fight this battle without a letup because the issue here is concerned with final values, the dignity of man, and

issue here is concerned with final values, the dignity of man, and the salvation of souls."

It is a body of moral thought with which our faculty seeks to enlighten the minds of individuals created in the image of God – with a rational intellect and a judgmental will – preparing them to assess correctly alternative directions of economic purpose and to choose ethically in the allocation of resources for advancing His Kingdom on Earth.

Paul C. Goelz, S.M., Ph.D.
Director
Algur H. Meadows Center
for Entrepreneurial Studies

St. Mary's University
of San Antonio

Acknowledgements

In pursuing our commitment to extend the cultural and professional horizons of our students as they strive to benefit humanity, the faculty of the School of Business and Administration is assisted substantially through the advice and assistance of the Advisory Council of Executives.

Rev. Charles W. Neumann, S.M., Professor of Theology at St. Mary's University, assisted in the editing of this manuscript.

Deep appreciation is extended to Louise Lagutchik for her exceptional competence and patient congeniality in overseeing the myriad of details involved with this Symposium and preparing this manuscript for publication.

Credo

The functional and institutional performance of the American economic system increases in complexity. The impact on the lives of individuals and our nation is direct and immediate. Along with this complexity, the dangers of confusion and error in policy formulation and resource allocation multiply exponentially.

St. Mary's University believes that educating the Renaissance Person for the Executive Suite will provide those qualities of moral perspective, conceptual analyses, and prudential decision-making which will perfect the economic order helping all of society to accomplish its great potential. To assist in fulfilling this mission our School of Business and Administration conducts International Symposia on the Philosophy of Free Enterprise through which individuals of high scholarship and proven performance analyze and articulate those Judeo-Christian values and philosophical concepts upon which the authentic character of a free people must be based.

It is our hope that these Symposia contribute meaningfully to advancing genuine freedom across the world.

Your appraisal of our efforts would assist us in fulfilling more effectively our dedication.

Rev. John A. Leies, S. M., S.T.D.
President

St. Mary's University
of San Antonio

ERIK RITTER VON
KUEHNELT-LEDDIHN

ERIK RITTER VON KUEHNELT-LEDDIHN

Erik Ritter von Kuehnelt-Leddihn is referred to by William F. Buckley, Jr. as "the world's most fascinating man." His repertoire as a linguist, author, lecturer, artist, and raconteur qualifies him eminently for this encomium.

Born in Austria he studied theology, civil and canon law at the University of Vienna, and later political science at the University of Budapest where he earned the Doctorate.

He speaks fluently eight languages and has a reading knowledge of eleven others. At sixteen he began to write for newspapers and periodicals, the first being the London *Spectator*, and at the age of twenty was sent to Russia as a special correspondent for a Hungarian daily.

In 1937 he taught at Georgetown University. After a visit to Spain during the Civil War he returned to the United States and was made head of the Department of History and Sociology at St. Peter's College in Jersey City. He taught Japanese at Fordham University. Later he joined the faculty of Chestnut Hill College in Philadelphia. In the summer of 1947 he resettled in Austria to devote himself to reading, writing, and further studies—visiting America every year since. He has regularly alternated periods of study with periods of travel to the Southern Hemisphere, the Subarctic, and around the world in order to gain first-hand information about every part of the globe.

Among his novels are *Gates of Hell, Night Over the East, Moscow 1979, Black Banners*, and *Die Gottlosen*, each published in various countries. His numerous theoretical writings include *Liberty or Equality?*, *America's Founding Fathers*, *Catholicism in America*, *Wanderwege*, *Lateinamerika*, *Zwischen Ghetto und Katakombe*, *From Sade and Marx to Hitler and Marcuse*, *Das Ratsel der Liebe*, and *Herz, Hirn und Ruckgrat* (illustrated with his own paintings).

In journalism he has written for many publications including: *America*, *The Catholic World*, *The Commonweal*, *The Geographic Review*, *Modern Age*, *Journal of Central European Affairs*, *The National Review* (for which he is foreign correspondent), *The Dublin Review*, *The Tablet*, *Frankfurter Hefte*, *Una Sancta*, *Humanitas* (Italy), *Criterio* (Argentina), *Credo* and *Samtid och Framtid* (Sweden), *Farmand* (Norway), *Seike* (Japan), and *Quadrant* and *The Advocate* (Australia).

His lectures cover the spectrum: "The Far-East Today," "Soviet Man Today," "The Five Wounds of Latin America," "Work Ethics and Commercialism: a World Problem," "What to Think of South Africa," "The Germans and the Germanies," and "The Irish Problem."

From all of this it is evident Dr. Kuehnelt-Leddihn dislikes specialization. He has repeatedly altered the line of his activities in order to attain and retain a comprehensive view of the humanities. Studies in political theory and practice have been largely directed toward finding ways to strengthen the great Western tradition of human freedom, now under attack from many sides. Recently his interests have been channeled toward the spiritual problem of Eros as distinguished from sex.

The Baron is married to Countess Christiane Goess (Ph.D.). They have three children and two grandchildren and live in a mountain village near the capital of the Austrian Tyrol. His hobbies are photography, hiking, music, bridge, stamp collecting, the writing of satirical essays, and painting. He had his first exhibition in 1971; and says he enjoys much more wielding the brush than the pen.

ECONOMICS IN THE CATHOLIC WORLD

Erik Ritter von Kuehnelt-Leddihn

Talking about economics in the Catholic World in the theoretical and practical sense means dealing with our Achilles Heel. Fortunately, this particular weakness is not crucial; it would be infinitely worse if our weakness were spiritual rather than material. Transcendence takes precedence over immanence. Diseases of the soul are more fatal than physical disabilities. Still, we have no right to be Manicheans: our bodies are not evil and need loving care.

THE EVOLUTION OF CATHOLIC ECONOMIC THOUGHT

Where does the nearly permanent and ubiquitous economic crisis of the *Orbis Catholicus* come from? Let us first look at the very roots of our Faith, at the Old Testament in which the Chosen People are shown as the foundation of the Incarnation. In the beginning they did not believe in immortality. The rather conservative Sadducees rejected, the more progressive Pharisees accepted, this notion. The Fourth Commandment, to honor one's parents "that thy days may be long upon the land which the Lord thy God has given thee," expresses the earlier belief which later yielded to further truths emerging gradually like objects on a photographic plate in the developer. Revelation is gradual. Wealth and health were originally very high values as proved in the story of Job and by the list of the four greatest curses: blindness, leprosy, childlessness and — *poverty*! The worship of Mammon does not yet figure as the worst menace.

All this changes with the advent of Christ, who by no means should be presented as a "radical revolutionary" so dear to the Leftist interpreters of our Faith. He is not the poor son of the humble carpenter. He is on His mother's, as well as on His putative father's side, descended from David to the Holy Virgin, "who knows no man"; the Archangel Gabriel emphasizes her Son's Davidic origin. She is related to Elizabeth and Zacharias, both Aaronites, and thus belongs to the highest social layers in Israel. Joseph has to go to Bethlehem for the census, because there he owns some real estate. The birth of the Savior in the stable is purely accidental. (A birth in the house of relatives, as P. Paul Gaechter has pointed out, would have caused very great ritualistic inconveniences to them.) We have countless pictures of the Magi who worship the child Jesus in the stable, beautiful paintings but strictly unbiblical because Scriptures tell us that the Wise Men paid homage to the Savior in "the house" (*oikia*), probably of Joseph who by then had built a house on his grounds. (And Joseph as *tekton* might have been not only a carpenter but architect as well. In any case wealth and status did not go automatically together.)

Christ was certainly not a "revolutionary." He told His hecklers to give to Caesar what is Caesar's and to God what belongs to God. Saint Paul is equally clear on this point. Our Lord emphasized the moral perils of riches, but in all likelihood it is not a camel which (in Matthew 19,24) is incapable of passing through the eye of a needle, but a string. Due to "itacism," the tendency in Greek to pronounce not only I, but also Y, EI, OI and ETA as an "ee" sound, *kamelos* was probably put down for *kamilos*. (The very ancient

Armenian Bible's translation uses "string"!) Nor was our Lord adverse to investments bringing dividends: note His parable of the talents – here the master says to the servant who returned his talent without increments – *Edei se oun balein ta argyria mou tois trapezitais?* "Why hast thou not given my money to the bankers?" These must have been in Biblical times foreigners, men from Syria (Aram) not subject to the Israelitic prohibitions of taking or giving interest for money lent or invested.

Our Lord moved freely in the society of the rich, as Josef Schmid in the *Regensburger Neues Testament* (Vol. II) pointed out, and when "social minded" Pharisees protested against the "waste" committed by Mary Magdalen using the expensive ointment which could have been sold for the benefit of the poor, Christ pointed out that His presence on earth was temporary, whereas the poor would always be with us. (The same Pharisaic argument is used today against beautiful churches.) Christ was certainly not an "anticapitalist," not a promoter of "social justice" or the totalitarian provider-state but of *charity*.

Our Lord, indeed, was not the "proletarian revolutionary" claimed by "Catholic leftists." He was not only of royal descent, but He also emphasized that He was a King (John 18,37). The Israelites saw in Him a prince of royal blood (they addressed Him frequently as "Son of David") and thus a pretender to the throne of Judea. He had the greatest difficulty impressing upon the people the fact that His kingdom was "not of this world." In Romanesque art Our Lord on the cross is a sovereign with a crown; only with the rise of the mendicant orders does this portrayal change so that He becomes the suffering crucified with a crown of thorns.

CHRISTIANS AND SOCIALISM

It has always been a temptation for Christianity to embrace socialism and socialist ideas. We hear of such efforts in the earliest days of the Church, in the first year after the landing of the Pilgrim Fathers, and today in the so-called "Liberation Theology" which is only thinly disguised Marxism with a sauce of arbitrarily chosen

Bible quotations torn out of their context. And we see it also in the phenomenon which I call in German, *Monastizismus*. It is the subject of an article which I published in Ortega's *Revista de Occidente* dealing with, among other things, the illegitimate effort to impose on everybody the monastic ideal of the sacrificial and voluntary surrender of God-given rights: personal freedom, married life, and property. The "Socialist Fatherland," the USSR, is, on the other hand, nothing but a godless monastery under a tyrannical abbot enforcing on those born within its walls the vows of obedience, poverty, and a puritanical way of life. There is, of course, also a whole "school" among Christians which does not want to fight poverty and romantically envisages a Christian society without rich people, even without a "bourgeois" middle class, where simply everybody is poor. Was not Christianity prior to its emancipation under Constantine the Great a religion of slaves, beggars, prostitutes, ham actors, and proletarians as Friedrich Engels suggested? The *Martyrologium Romanum* shows that the Christian Faith quickly reached the highest social and intellectual layers in antiquity, and Adolph von Harnack pointed out in his *Militia Christi* that Christianity was especially successful in the Roman Army. (Pacifists, please take note!)

USURY

The economic development of the Christian West had been hampered for a long time by the Old Testament prohibition against taking interest (Leviticus, 25, 35-37). It figures in the writings of the Schoolmen as "usury." Thomas Aquinas himself, so thoroughly influenced by "*the* Philosopher," by Aristotle, also took the stand of the Stagirite who flatly declared that money does not beget money like domestic animals begetting offspring. Therefore, during most of the Middle Ages only the Israelitic community was permitted to lend money with interest which they did – to Christians. In *De Regimine Principum* (Part II) St. Thomas took a very dim view of the merchant who bought goods and sold them at a higher price. He only made an exception for traders who, for patriotic reasons, imported merchandise from far away countries which otherwise could not be obtained. Herein we also see the aristocratic outlook of the Aquinate, a close relative of Frederick II, the *Stupor Mundi*. It was, in addition, remembered by Christians east and west that the only people physically chastized by Our Lord had been merchants. Thus banking and trading had little social appeal in the Middle Ages. It was not the royal road to excellence.

Still, by the Fifteenth Century a change could be observed. Various arguments in favor of business were raised and the prohibition against so-called usury was quite legitimately circumvented. This new attitude was mainly seen in Italy as well as in Spain, in France, and in Southern Germany. Marjorie Grice-Hutchinson, a disciple of F. A. von Hayek, has written profusely about free enterprise in "reconquered" Spain. A Franciscan, Fra Luca Pacioli di Borgo, invented before 1500 the method of double-entry bookkeeping, and North Italian traders and bankers came to London where they settled on Lombard Street. Many of our banking expressions therefore are Italian. "Capitalism," to use this Marxist expression, was indeed born in Catholic Europe. It received, however, an added impetus through the Reformation.

THE WORK ETHIC

Why did this happen? The Reformation reemphasized the Bible (which, by the way, had already appeared in many handwritten and printed German translations), and with it the notion from the Old Testament was revived that riches are a sign of God's special favor. Luther and even far more so Calvin believed in predestination, which implied for them, that the Elect were already visibly blessed (with riches) during their lifetime. Therefore, the good Calvinist made every effort to prove to himself and to his fellow men that he was certain of his salvation. He worked hard and avoided a luxurious life. This attitude also led to Puritanism.

Max Weber (whose magisterial works were translated into English only after World War II) has shown us the reasons for the economic supremacy of the countries of the Reformation compared with the Catholic nations (and, incidentally, the regions where the Eastern Church prevailed). He did not fail to emphasize even the material superiority of the Calvinist over the Lutheran element and was able to give statistical proofs of the validity of his thesis. His stress was on free enterprise and the disappearance of all laws against "usury," yet in my opinion he should have primarily emphasized the stronger work ethic.

These developments were greatly enhanced by the fact that both leading Reformation faiths abolished the veneration of the Saints, which resulted in the abolition of their feasts. Prior to the Reformation the calendar abounded everywhere with holy days of obligation averaging in Western Europe (including the Sundays) between 130 and 150. Work was forbidden on these days, and in most countries also work by artificial light. (The guilds enforced this through surveillance by flying commissions.) In the Calvinist world even the celebration of Christmas was considered to be a sign of "Popery," and in Scotland Christmas was a workday until early this century. I have a copy of a handbill printed in the early Eighteenth Century in Massachusetts in which celebrating the Birth of Our Lord was threatened with a fine of 5 shillings, a considerable sum at that time.

In other words, the "Protestant Work Ethic" with its discipline and a controlling community spirit triumphed in Northern Europe while workaholics did not abound in Catholic countries. The Opus Dei eventually sprang up in Spain because that country badly needed the idea of the sanctification of work. The Basque Provinces gave birth to the Jesuit order because its people realized where the lack of discipline might lead. Yet the mendicant orders, while themselves not alien to work, had psychologically prepared the world for begging. (When a fourth hour of manual work was introduced in one of these orders, a howl of indignation went up.) Let us note here that originally even the Jesuits during their novitiate had to make a pilgrimage to Rome, begging their way to the Eternal City. Begging was also encountered in Europe's North, but there it was looked down on: the poor had to be ashamed of themselves. Needless to say, begging became a scourge in England immediately after the break with Rome when all the monasteries, all the Catholic institutions of charity had disappeared. Hordes of mendicants then swarmed all over the country. In Catholic Southern Europe, however, begging retained its status. Earlier in this century Professor Allison Peers was approached by a beggar in the streets of Madrid with these words: *Hermanito, una limosna por el amor de Dios, que en la plenitud de mi juventud me had quitado la gana de trabajar.* "Dear brother, give me an alms for the love of God who in the fullness of my youth took away from me the disposition for work." Well, how does one become well-to-do in a society which is not work-directed? In Guatemala City there are over 10,000 licensed (and only Heaven knows how many unlicensed) lottery ticket vendors. This tallies with the Irish Sweepstakes and Bingo in the United States. "Windfalls" seem to be sinful on the contrary in the *Orbis Reformatus* where games of chance are tolerated merely in the sign of "permissiveness" and not in good conscience.

DISCIPLINE AND LA DOLCE VITA

It is obvious that the lack of hard work, a dreamy imagination, open delight in the good things (from a refined cuisine to painting, music, and architecture) do not make for much discipline. Technology, too, needs discipline and sobriety of thought. It is not so curious a fact that in large parts of Europe the color black is symbolic for the Catholic Church and Anarchism. The World of the Reformation is evolutionary, the Catholic World, however, is revolutionary. "Rum, Romanism, and Rebellion" go well together, as Americans have found out. Thus the living standards in the Reformed countries are higher than the lands of the Old Church: England or Scotland are richer than Ireland, Scandinavia is richer than Spain, Ontario is richer than Quebec, the United States wealthier than Latin America, and Switzerland is more prosperous than Austria. Yet, high living standards do not automatically make for a better quality of life. Tourism in Europe goes from the North to the South. The *dolce vita* is not characteristic of Finland. Nobody in his right mind would open an English, Scottish, or Prussian restaurant in Manhattan. It highlights the economic situation that in 1930 of the six Regents of the *Banque de France* five were Calvinists, one was a Hebrew, and none a Catholic. Louis Salleron in his *Les Catholiques et le Capitalisme* (Paris, 1952) tells us that, to the French, banks were always "juives et protestantes." The Anglicans and Presbyterians are still the "cat's whiskers" in the Republic of Ireland where their material superiority has more than historical-political causes. This ought theoretically to reassure "Protestants" in Northern Ireland, fearful of reunion, yet their fears and hatreds have reasons much subtler than merely economic. Belfast is assuredly richer than Dublin, but I would rather be buried in Dublin than live in Belfast.

It is a fact that the high work ethic born in Northwestern Europe has only slowly moved in an eastern and southern direction and has never reached Russia where Marxism has nipped individual initiative in the bud and material motivation is non-existent. Hence the extremely low living standards. This is also demonstrated by the fact that the farmers of the United States (3% of the population) feed a large part of the world, but the collectivized Soviet peasants (27%) fail to nourish even the USSR. And it is also true that Christians in the Near East and in Southern Asia will prosper far more than their Islamic and Hindu neighbors. This is evident in Lebanon, in Egypt, in India, and most markedly in Cyprus where the Christian Greek South faces the Mohammedan-Turkish North. A glance at dissected Nicosia shows this clearly.

LIBERALISM

Certain things we Catholics should learn from the *Orbis Reformatus*. But there are obstacles to overcome. One of these is the still vivid memory of the old feud between the Church and genuine liberalism. What since the 1930's is called "liberalism" in America has nothing to do with the "real McCoy": it is moderate leftism and watered down socialism. There are, as a matter of fact, four phases of genuine liberalism. The political term "liberal" itself is Spanish and was coined in 1812 for the supporters of the Constitution of Cadiz. Southey used it in 1816 in its Spanish form and wrote "our British *liberales*."

There is "Pre-Liberalism," represented by Adam Smith who, having died in 1790, never used the term. Pre-Liberalism was rather commercial. Then came Early Liberalism, represented by men like de Tocqueville, Montalembert, Acton, and Jacob Burckhardt. The first three were Catholic aristocrats. Burckhardt, a patrician from Basel, was a famous historian. Their interests were rather political and social than economic.[1]

The third phase, after Pre-Liberalism and Early Liberalism, we can call Old Liberalism, and with this kind of Liberalism, the Church had real difficulties. The old liberals did not just hark back to Pre-Liberalism but also were only too often philosophical relativists. They were (and are) skeptical toward the concept of absolute truth, hostile to "organized religion" and especially to dogmatic convictions. They never carefully distinguished between tolerance (which is compatible with dogmatism) and indifference. They were undoubtedly the ones anathematized by the *Syllabus*. Here we also have to bear in mind that the conservative parties of the past had usually an aristocratic and agrarian leadership with no love lost for the now rising class of manufacturers, traders, and bankers, and thus demanded that the latter take care of the old or disabled employees as the patriarchal landowner did of his landworkers and servants. This obviously was unfeasible. The liberal-conservative antagonism had thus a religious as well as a social-political dimension in which the Church was ideologically driven to the conservative side. (This is even true of Europe's North. The final break between William II and Bismarck happened when the former sided with working class demands.) The appearance of socialism complicated the situation which thus at the end of the last century became "triangular."

The Old Liberals in turn were followed by the New Liberals

who not only thought highly of the Early Liberals but also strongly valued the Christian tradition, men and women like Wilhelm Roepke, Walter Eucken, Alexander Ruestow, Daniel Villey, Goetz Briefs, Karl Brandt, and Heddy Neumeister. On account of far-reaching differences the surviving luminaries (Eucken had died in 1951) left the Mont-Pelerin Society in 1961 in a dramatic move. In 1963 they met in Augsburg for two days with spokesmen of the Catholic Faith (all priests with one exception). The New Liberals provided for this encounter only two Catholic representatives — the unforgettable Goetz Briefs and my humble self. A Dominican who had written a flaming indictment of the New Liberals in a king-size volume opened the attack but found out to his horror that he had believed all members of the Mont-Pelerin Society to be New Liberals. Those cited and censored in his book were in fact mostly Old Liberals. He knew nothing about the schism and remained silent all through the long sessions.

INADEQUATE STUDY OF ECONOMICS

Besides theology our Catholic thinkers too often study only such disciplines as sociology and psychology but rarely economics, a most mysterious file of intellectual endeavor. Compared with economics, theology appears like a clear, unequivocal natural science. Economics is, indeed, a science where fools rush in and angels fear to tread. With depressing frequency I have watched eminent theologians, philosophers, psychologists, and novelists pontificating about economics without any preparation whatever. (I myself did it like an idiot at the age of 22 in my novel *Gates of Hell!*) Jacques Maritain praised the "atheistic Communists" for having "abolished the profit motive." (He deeply influenced Archbishop Montini, who became Pope Paul VI.) A Papal Legate, now a Cardinal, visiting Havana of all places, declared that: "We too have studied Marx and learned a lot from him!" (What on earth? Marx' antisemitism? His contempt for the workers? His patent economic ignorance?) The Dominican Father Lebret, largely responsible for the Encyclical *Populorum Progressio*, visiting a seminary in São Paulo, confessed that he thought God to be rather on the side of the Communists than of the capitalists. "And if you ask me now, whether I am unhappy about this, I have to tell you that I am not."

THE PROBLEMS OF LATIN AMERICA

Latin America and its economic as well as socio-political condition deeply worries many a responsible Catholic. There are the masses of the poor and a tiny minority of very rich people, creating great social and political tensions. This is an area most important to the Church because, due to the high birthrate the majority of Catholic Christians will be living there at the beginning of the next century. The abyss between rich and poor, on the other hand, is typical for all countries where poverty and even misery prevail. These countries have, as a rule, a curious social pyramid characterized by a very broad base which suddenly shrinks to a very high and conspicuous needle. The reason for this state of affairs is simply a general laziness, inertia, a lack of enthusiasm for systematic work, and a non-acquisitive spirit combined with the extraordinary zeal of small, intelligent minorities who encounter little competition. Such great discrepancy in wealth the economically ignorant layman will inevitably explain by "exploitation," and the remedy he will almost always propose is "social justice," which means confiscation and redistribution. Yet, if we break off the admittedly very provocative needle, melt it down and pour it over the base, no change will be observed. In 1958 a very careful German investigation was made to see what would happen if all incomes above 1,000 Marks a month were to be confiscated and these sums put into a jackpot and every federal citizen given an equal share. It would have amounted to 14 Pfennig *per diem*. (These sums could today be multiplied by 5; one Mark today is roughly equal to 50 cents.) Now, in Latin America such an experiment would be infinitely more abortive and senseless. It would destroy a culturally and economically most productive layer of society without benefitting the masses.

SOCIAL ENGINEERING

In conversation an eminent theologian known worldwide, while insisting on "Social Justice" for Latin America involving a radical redistribution freely admitted that, economically, such naive social engineering would be perfect nonsense. However, he went on to point out that there is another aspect to the problem, a spiritual one: the temptation of envy and jealousy. These are sins he said, and as a Catholic priest he is obliged to combat the occasion of sin. Therefore, he stands for expropriation. I answered him with a parable. There are two sisters: Isabel and Heloise. Isabel is beautiful and enjoys the courtship of countless young men. Heloise is an ugly duckling who attracts not a single male and cries every night in her pillow. Should we now take a sharp knife and scratch up the face of Isabel? For then Heloise would no longer be envious and jealous. The theologian gave no answer but merely threw up his hands in despair and horror.

In Latin America, especially in the racially mixed north, we see not only poverty (which need not be deplored) but misery, which is really bad. (It is important to distinguish between both situations, as one can be poor, but not miserable, and happy.) The reason for this lamentable state of affairs is not so much Iberians, but Indian indifference to work. We have to remember that the Spaniards and the Portuguese were forced to import African slaves because the Indians, brutally forced to work by the Aztec and Mayan kings as well as by the Incas, failed to respond to their new masters in the *encomienda* system. Moreover, we are not faced there by an acquisitive society which wants to "get ahead." To make matters worse there is not only alcoholism and drug abuse but also the enormous weakening of the family due to machismo, the male conceit in sexual and even more so in procreative activity. Children, even illegitimate ones, are a matter of male pride, with the result that in central and northern South America the percentage of illegitimate births occasionally rises up to 85 percent. (I was once introduced to the deputy of a Central American republic, a man belonging to the upper class, who boasted that his father had provided him with 103 brothers and sisters.) Under these circumstances it can hardly be expected that, in such purely matrilineal societies, where the mother has to work hard for her brood, the grandmother would not have authority enough to send the children to school or to incite them to honest work. Without an intact family everything is bound to go awry.

ERRORS IN EMPHASIS

Here another specific failure of the Latin American Church in the past must be taken into account. She did not preach the "natural virtues" with sufficient emphasis. The Church only too often put the accent on the Faith and rarely praised sufficiently such ethic prescriptions as chastity, diligence, sobriety, truthfulness, concern for the family, frugality, respect for life and property — virtues which the Left might consider *bourgeois* but which are nevertheless essential for a good society. It is a sad fact that it is not our Church but the North-American sects evangelizing these areas who always put stress on morals. And what is a large sector of the Latin American Church doing now? Like a monkey in the jungle she is swinging from the tree of semi-superstitious folkloric marginalities to the tree of the so-called "Liberation Theology" which leads to no liberation whatsoever but to great poverty and to the omnipotent red state of Muscovite inspiration. Here the grossest economic ignorance is at work.

EXPLOITATION

Is "exploitation" at the root of all these evils? Talking to a South American priestly defender of Liberation Theology which not only has a Marxist kernel, but also harbors distinctly heretical ideas, I told him point-blank: "You seem to see the situation of what you call 'capitalism' in the following way: There is a prison cell with four inmates. Three of them are little thieves, the fourth, on the other hand, is a strong and tough multiple-murderer. He takes away half of the portions of the other three and thus gets stronger while the others get weaker and weaker." "Exactly," said the priest with shining eyes. "You could not better describe the situation in our allegedly free world!" "But, my dear friend," I replied, "there is no analogy whatsoever between such a prison cell with four jail-birds and a free economy in a free society. In the cell are four stomachs, four walls, and a lavatory. In a free economy with collective bargaining – trade unions with responsible, Christian leaders, after all, do exist – the high salaries of the directors and the dividends of the shareholders hardly affect the well-being of the working class adversely. They indeed occasionally earn a lot but what can they do with their money? They will certainly not bury it. They either give it to a bank or spend it. The bank invests it or gives loans to other people, and the money spent for whatever purpose, including the buying of luxury goods, benefits other enterprisers and their workers or buys services. These monies go through countless arteries into every part of society."

The priest hesitated a moment: "But if these sums are transferred abroad, if they finally land in the United States or in Switzerland...."

"They benefit workers in other climes," I replied, "and they would not land there if they could be safely invested in their countries of origin, if 'EXPROPRIATION' would not be written with flaming letters on the banners of every leftist movement and would not form part of the program of murderous guerilla priests, who, instead of anointing the sick, oil their submachine guns of National Liberation Fronts or Liberation Theologies that frighten the local enterprisers and effectively deter foreign investors. This, precisely, is the tragedy of the Third World...."

"What do you want the Church to do? To preach something like a practical materialism? This is not really our task!"

"The Accion Popular in Colombia does it quite well, but instead priests give sermons on politics, economics, sociology, and psychology so that simple minded Catholics who want to hear about God's revealed word join sects because there they find preachers who refer to the eternal truth in Scriptures."

The good man fell silent because he knew about this leakage. Of course, in his economic naivete he does not stand alone. There is, for instance, a psychologist whose ideas Arthur Koestler considered to be barbarous trivialities leading us back to the Dark Ages: Professor Burrhus F. Skinner, a "Behaviorist" who declared that when people own or acquire something it is only "at the expense of poverty, disease, and filth for many more." If this were true we could not sit down to dinner.

We can hardly find much consolation in the fact that in the other Christian Churches the confusion about the Third World is just as great as with us – if not greater. The World Council of Churches has methodically financed terrorism in large parts of Africa. With subsidies from Geneva, Mugabe trained his terrorists who not only murdered but mutilated peaceful Shonas and Ndebeles in order to strike fear into the hearts of "collaborators": they cut off noses, ears, and lips of its victims. An "Emergency Committee of Evangelicals in Germany" has collected funds to finance cosmetic operations on these beastially disfigured black Rhodesians. One's mind stands still. At least, we Catholics *so far* have not had to face such issues.

AN ECONOMIC "THIRD WAY"

Still, we often have been foolish about economic issues in the realm of theory as well as of practice. (The Vatican itself has shown often incredible ineptitude and credulity in handling its finances.) These are facts which have to be faced squarely and should not be swept under the carpet. To say that the children of darkness are more clever than the children of light does not absolve us from our responsibilities. Today after the death of Goetz Briefs and Daniel Villey we have hardly one economist of worldwide renown in the ranks of practicing Catholics. Sometimes one encounters economic illusions in the highest ecclesiastic circles. I was deeply impressed by Dom Helder Camara, the Archbishop of Recife, as a person. He struck me as a holy and sincere man, but his economics were another matter. He thought that the

Yugoslav economic system was a worthwhile example to follow. But that country lives on Western handouts and even so is on the brink of total bankruptcy. There is the age-old Catholic dream of an economic "Third Way," of an order between free enterprise and Marxist state capitalism, but "there ain't no sich animal." The means of production either belong to private individuals, to groups of private owners, or to the State which Nietzsche had called *das kaelteste aller Ungeheuser*, "the coldest of all monsters."

Free enterprise fosters inequalities and there is an egalitarian temptation in all of Christianity, but we all are unequal in every respect and, above all, in the eyes of God. If Judas Iscariot were equal to St. John the Baptist, Christianity could close shop. Some theologians play tricks by arguing adverbially that we all *equally* have bodies, *equally* have souls, and *equally* are called for salvation, but the Rockefellers and I *equally* have banking accounts though our banking accounts are not *equal*. *Eleutheria*, freedom, is mentioned in the Bible again and again, but not *isotes*, and when the latter word occurs it does not have the sense of equality, but only of equity. Here fashionable political notions have entered theology ignoring Romans 12,2: "Do not conform to the *aion* (which means time and world). It is not equality that is justice, but Ulpian's *suum cuique* "to each his due." Still the Trojan asses of the theological *demi-monde*, clamoring for the consensus of the masses, want it differently. They apparently ache for the Provider State. Yet Pius XII warned them already way back in 1952 when he spoke about ". . . the protection of the individual and the family from an all-embracing socialization, a process in whose terminal stage the terrifying vision of the Leviathan State would become a gruesome reality. The Church is going to fight this battle without a letup because the issue here is concerned with final values, the dignity of man, and the salvation of souls."

CONCLUSION

Certain voices in our midst are seemingly crying in the wilderness. There is, for instance, the famous French Dominican

Raymond Bruckberger who recently added to his series of startling books one called *Capitalisme-mais c'est la vie* (Capitalism-But This Is Life), Paris, 1983. I do not like the use of the Marxist term "capitalism," but I must confess that this is a splendid book. Of course, his ideas are not too popular, not "timely" as socialism is thought to be in its various eastern and western forms. But socialism is a *fausse idee claire*, a clear but false idea explainable to any junior high school student in 12 minutes, that in no time has conquered half the world. Christianity needed three-hundred years to prevail. (And to explain the Free Market System to somebody I would prescribe several weeks in a seminar.)

Of course, in the meantime the economic gap between the Catholic world and the regions of the Reformation churches has shrunk. *One* of the several reasons for this development is the ethical demoralization through the Provider State (wrongly called the welfare state) in northern Europe. (I know German and Scandinavian entrepreneurs who prefer Spanish to native workers.) The per capital GNP of Austria is higher than that of Britain. Catholics now play a major role in German and French banking or in Dutch department store ownership. In the United States the Sociology Institute of the University of Chicago has told us that Americans of Catholic Irish ancestry form the relatively highest income group followed by the Catholics of German stock. Group three are the Hebrews with WASPS taking the fourth place. In view of the Catholic mentality this was, indeed, a stiff up-hill fight.

The great menace of our time, however, is collectivism in its various forms. The spirit of our times, of the *aion*, is anti-personalism favoring the servile state, favoring Leviathan. In the battle against it we ought to get all the strength we can from our Faith. After all, Chesterton told us that the Church alone protects us from the degrading servitude of being children of our times.

FOOTNOTE

[1]When the prestigious Mont-Pelerin Society which comprised Old and New Liberals was formed in 1947 in a hotel near Vevey, Switzerland, two leaders, the Old Liberal F. A. Hayek and the New Liberal Wilhelm Roepke, proposed to call it the "De Tocqueville-Acton Society." Thereupon Professor Frank Knight of the University of Chicago violently protested because these were "Roman Catholic Aristocrats." Therefore, they chose the name of the mountain just visible through the window. Yet, the nobility was always interested in freedom, and the leadership of the highly liberal Austrian School of Economics, with the exception of the late Fritz Machlup, consisted solely of noblemen—Menger, Wieser, Böhm-Bawerk, Mises, Hayek, and Haberler.

FORUM

S. THOMAS GREENBURG   LOUIS H. STUMBERG   ROBERT V. WEST, JR.

PANELISTS

S. Thomas Greenburg

S. Thomas Greenburg earned his Doctorate in Philosophy at Columbia University. Honorary Doctorates have been conferred on him by St. Edward's University, St. John's University, Molloy College, and the Royal Academy of St. Theodora. He has been President of two colleges spanning twenty years. In the early Eighties he was Research Professor at St. Mary's University. For several years he conducted a weekly television program on the Great Books. Dr. Greenburg's published works include pamphlets on "The Identity Crisis in Catholic Higher Education"; "The Challenge to the Free Enterprise Philosophy"; and "The Challenge to the Church's Authority." Published books are *The Concept of Infinity*; *A Symposium on the Magisterium: A Positive Statement*; *Free Enterprise: An Enterprise in Freedom*; and *Sapientia Christiana*. Dr. Greenburg continues as President of the Institute of Christian Higher Education.

Louis H. Stumberg

Mr. Louis H. Stumberg, a graduate of the University of Texas, has had a distinguished executive career. He served as Vice Chairman of Del Monte USA, Civilian Aide to the Secretary of the Army, Member of the Governor's Water Task Force; and Mayor of Terrell Hills, Texas. Mr. Stumberg is an Elder in the First Presbyterian Church. His Banking service is as Director and member of the Executive Committee of National Bancshares of Texas and Director of NBC Bank of San Antonio. Public service includes the Board of Trustees of Trinity University, The University of Texas at San Antonio Development Board, Director of the San Antonio Community of Churches, Director of the United Way of San Antonio, Past Chairman of the Greater San Antonio Chamber of Commerce, Past President of the Alamo Area Council of the Boy Scouts of America, and Past President of the Rotary Club. Mr. Stumberg also serves as Vice Chairman of the Sportsmen's Clubs of Texas, Director of Game Conservation International, and was a member of the Texas Parks & Wildlife Commission.

Robert V. West, Jr.

Dr. Robert V. West, Jr. is the Founder and Chairman of Tesoro Petroleum Corporation, a large energy company with extensive international operations. He has invested his time and talents in a broad spectrum of local and national service activities. He is on the Board of Trustees of St. Mary's University. Internationally he founded the Caribbean/Central American Action in Washington, D.C., a non-profit organization; he is also a Director of the Americas Society. Awards include "The International Citizen of the Year Award" conferred by the World Affairs Council of San Antonio; the "People of Vision Award" from the National Society for the Prevention of Blindness; and the "Good Scout Award" by the Boy Scouts of America. Dr. West's knowledge of world-wide economic conditions is distilled from extensive travel and study of nations and their peoples.

Wealth and Poverty in Other Lands

Question: Both Mr. Stumberg and Dr. West have traveled across the world, and particularly in Third World countries. What I would like to ask them is: In your experience, Dr. West in the Caribbean as well as South America; and

Mr. Stumberg in Outer Mongolia; what are
these peoples' perception of wealth and poverty?

We have our own perception of wealth and
poverty.

What are the causes of wealth and how do
you create wealth; what are the causes of
poverty?

Do you see any difference in the perceptions
of wealth and poverty in these countries relative to ours?

Louis Stumberg:

That is an interesting matter. I just returned from going through
Russia and into Mongolia and China. It had been eighteen years
since I had been in Russia, and I have a few perceptions that I
would like to share with you; some of the things that I observed.

Russia probably has the most rigid society that you could
encounter. When they talk about the freedom of the individual in
Russia and the fact that everybody is equal, that is the biggest
deception. I will give you some examples.

There are three types of stores: the store that everybody shops
in, the hard currency store, and then the store that only the big
politicians shop in. One of the best things that you can get is a card
to shop at that last store. Why? They have everything in the world
there. They don't have to pay the politicians but six thousands dollars a year when they can go in there and buy for virtually nothing. The hard currency store is the one that I or any foreigner
could shop at. People do not take Russian rubles there. If the individual Russian can get some hard currency, he can shop there.
Then there is the other store, where everybody shops; where
there are many shortages. There are no shortages in the hard currency store; there are not shortages in the top store.

You drive down the main boulevard, and there is one line of traffic in the center; each side, that is reserved. It is reserved for big politicians who drive along in a closed limousine with the curtains closed; and nobody else drives in that center lane.

So that is what we mean when we talk about a rigid society.

I think that one of the things that has always interested me in Free Enterprise is how we try to relate Free Enterprise to this country. Everything is in comparison to us.

I have just come from China. Ten years ago China was a nation on the verge of starvation, a major importer of grain. What happened in ten years? They instituted some Free Enterprise into the Chinese economy. People had never had the opportunity to market their own products; the individual seller on the street was not there; and they were on the verge of starvation all the time. In ten years under the present administration China has not only become self-sufficient in agricultural needs but they are a small net exporter. Where they were looking for a bowl of rice, they are now looking for a television set. Expectations have changed. No longer do they sit on the verge of starvation.

They are now beginning under Free Enterprise and I look at Free Enterprise and capitalism as not just things; it is the right for me, with my experience and my education, to deploy that capital wherever I see fit. That is the way I see Free Enterprise, and the right to make that capital pay dividends to me.

When they realized that in China, that they could plow their fields and see a return and raise their buffalo and cattle and their chickens and see a return, it became one of the spikes that has driven American agriculture to the wall.

In India they are doing the same thing. They have begun to realize that and now they let the farmers have a right to the return on what they produce; India now is a net exporter.

I ask myself: Where will the farmer be if Russia finally wakes up to the fact that they can release that same energy and become totally self-sufficient, as probably they once were when they had much more freedom.

I relate that to you because when I was in Russia, there was an oppressive feeling all the time. You never know whom you are talking to. I could not turn to Dr. West and say something that I felt. Why? Because five percent or so of the people in Russia are informers. Every apartment manager, every businessman or merchant can easily be a KGB informer. They pay them a bonus when they turn somebody in.

Of the buildings that are going up in Moscow, the biggest one is the new KGB headquarters. Why? Because that is the only way to keep that society under control. It is stronger than the army.

People working under that type of oppressive environment cannot function, cannot respond, cannot produce. The society gives a lot of respect to the arts, and they produce some great artists because they allow those people to be creative. But outside of that, the society is virtually completely bound, extremely bound.

When I went into Mongolia, not having been there for eighteen years, I saw many changes.

You ask how do they view property. In Mongolia they are allowed to have a herd of cattle, a herd of camels, a herd of sheep, and they are allowed to sell them. The result? Population has gone up, people dress better, and they live far better than the Russians because they have a lot more individual right to deploy their capital.

In Russia, you have identification but that does not say you can go all over Russia. In some cases it is limited just to Moscow, and in other cases you may be able to go somewhere else. But just because you are a Russian citizen does not mean you can go where you wish. That is not true at all.

When people cannot utilize their own capital, minds, experience, you are not going to get a high type of production, you are not going to get a high type of creative ability.

You ask why is Russia then so great in the military? Simple. They put so much of their resources into that. The individual that is a great scientist has one of those cars. That is their incentive – to move up to where you can shop at the company store, so to speak. You have a country house. They have incentive systems, don't kid yourselves. For the ones that they really want, they give them incentive; they can get a chauffeur to drive them, but for the common people they get shoddy products, and there is little or no reason for them to do anything.

But there has been a basic change in eighteen years. It used to be that no one at the hotel could take a tip, and service was rotten eighteen years ago. We had waiters that would not wait on you. What happened? Today they can take tips. We put a bunch of coins on the table. Every time the waiter came, my friends and I would push him one. You cannot believe the way the service improved. Now that you can tip them, service in those type of places has improved. Why? Because there is an incentive to do a better job.

Every bit of it applies to what we are talking about, the ability of human beings to be rewarded for what they do. When you take that away from them, you are going to get exactly what you are paying for, not a nickel more.

Robert West:
    I want to respond to the question, which was: How do people in other parts of the world perceive wealth and poverty?

    I have had the good fortune, as Louis has had, to travel widely in the world. I have not had the time in Russia he has. I have been to Russia but not to really spend any time there. I have been in some of the other Iron Curtain countries, where I have found the same things in those countries to which Louis refers.

    I would say, in answer to your question, that the perception of almost every place I have been—and I will define "wealth" and not "poverty" because, needless to say, "poverty" would be the opposite of this—the perception of wealth is the opportunity to participate in an economic system that is comparable to that which they believe from their exposure exists in the U.S.A.

    Almost every place I have been around the world, it is the economic system and economic opportunities that exist in the U.S. that really stand out and command the attention of the people and command their respect. I spent six days in China and three in Peking and three in Shanghai, and that is the limit of my exposure to what I saw the Chinese people to be; and they admire Free Enterprise. People everywhere that I have been admire Free Enterprise. They admire the American tradition and way of life, not necessarily the glossy way of life that some of our people may manifest but the way of life with freedom of opportunity.

To the people whom I have met, particularly in the Caribbean region and South America, the opportunity to work in a creative manner and to have an upward mobility opportunity in their work: that is their perception of "wealth." It is not necessarily measured in their minds in terms of absolute dollars, whether they make $100,000 or $200,000 a year or whatever, but if they have a position, a job, are able to work and have employment in a Free Enterprise system that offers them upward mobility; that to many, many people is their perception of "wealth."

"Poverty" would be the deprivation of not having that opportunity.

Louis Stumberg:

It is my experience that people want to work and do not want a handout and do not want the kind of dictated handouts that one has in a dictatorial system, be it far left or far right. I have always found there are lazy people everywhere and in every society but I have found most people really want to work, and one of the things Erik mentioned a minute or so ago is that there is no poverty – and I don't think you said it just exactly like this, but this is my paraphrase – where there is a work ethic.

I have found in general that most people around the world want to work and are willing to work, given the opportunity and given the economic and political circumstances that create that opportunity.

Freedom and the Drug Economy

Question: I would like either panelist to comment on what my experience has been in the last year since moving to the city of Miami.

The newspapers report variously that somewhere between forty-five and as much as sixty percent of our economy in south Florida is related to drugs, that the visible industry simply cannot sustain the wealth that is invisible.

How do we and what do we do to restrain the kind of freedom which prevails there from catering to the baseness, the crassness of life, the most destructive kinds of entrepreneurial skills? And they are good at it, so much so that we have entire police departments in jail – the city of Opa Locka, twenty-nine officers and the mayor are presently in jail, not only having been indicted but convicted.

What do we do to address that? Is it just freedom to participate?

Robert West:

I do not think you can have unlimited freedom without discipline, and that is what is going on, in my opinion; a lack of sufficient discipline in the use of drugs.

I think the only answer to the drug problem – and I will agree with you that it is a disaster, not only to south Florida but throughout the entire country; I think all that can be done there as well as throughout the country is to control the consumption. You cannot control the production of drugs in Colombia or Bolivia or Mexico or anywhere else.

We ought to enact laws that are onerous and punish severely the drug commerce, the drug users and the drug distributors. We can put an end to it that way. We have to choke off the consumption, and that will put an end to this drug economy that exists in south Florida.

You mentioned twenty-nine police officers and the mayor of Opa Locka were convicted of dealing in drugs. You may recall a couple of years ago that the prime minister of one of the Caribbean islands was convicted for his participation in drugs; and I assume, by the length of his sentence, he soon will be returned to society also.

I think this participation in the drug economy is going on throughout the entire lower band of the whole Western Hemisphere because they do not want to quit, and that is because they do not have other means of economic support, the countries of which I am speaking, such as Bolivia and Colombia, than supplying these drugs.

I do not know if you read in *The Wall Street Journal* a couple of days ago about the enterprising pilot who was forty-five or fifty years old and was flying a little twin-engine Aztec to bring in his cargo to the United States, along with which there came three or four hundred kilos of cocaine. I ran some quick mathematical calculations in my mind, and one trip, which you can make in one night, if you don't mind being shot at as you land and take off, is worth about $700,000. That is just to get it into this country, before it gets involved in all this distribution network.

The only thing that we can do is to crack down on the consumption. Many people are afraid to do that today. There is a lot of discussion in our press whether or not city employees would or would not take tests for drugs.

We are giving consideration to that in our company right now. We have people in our company who think we should give them only for people working in "hazardous occupations"; I personally do not feel that way. There is concern on the part of people feeling that we are infringing on the rights of other people and their freedom of choice. But, in my judgment, having a receptionist sitting in the hall using cocaine is no more acceptable to me than having a pilot under the influence of cocaine fly an airplane.

We have to crack down on consumption, and I think if we do not stop it, it ultimately is going to corrupt our entire society – our children, our economy. Where it has changed the economy, that will have a political effect because of the amount of money that is generated from illicit sales and distribution of drugs; they will buy the police forces, as you said, and higher, members of Congress or governors, and ultimately, it is not a wild assumption, I suppose, that the drug money could influence the national political area.

I think the point at which to get rid of drugs is at the point of consumption.

Sidney Greenburg:

May I see if I understand? There is another part to the gentleman's question that was not identified in the response. I think he was using the drug example as an example, but that is not the essence of the question. The question relates to the false use and illegal use of capitalism, the evil use, the irresponsible use, as sometimes seen in the drug traffic, et cetera. That is what I think you are driving at, and therefore, there has to be some evaluation of and distinction made between Free Enterprise as a positive, with its responsibilities, and not reducing it to a criminal notion of profit.

Response:

That is the real question.

Sidney Greenburg:

The problem is the misuse of the system and philosophy that we think is so great; that has to be taken care of. That is the sort of thing we need to address.

Louis Stumberg:

Our company operates all over the world. We have had our operations in the Philippines; you name it.

You are always exposed to corruption because in many of these countries that is the nature of the reality.

You have a responsibility, in my opinion, as a businessman or a businesswoman or a business, to operate in an ethical, in a morally defensible, and in a legal manner; period!

Our company made us sign a statement each year that we had not bribed anybody and that we had not involved ourselves—I am talking about at the upper levels—in any way that did not meet those standards.

If you operate with those standards, I assure you, you won't be dealing in drugs.

I do not think that Free Enterprise gives anybody a license to steal or corrupt; period! Now, anytime that anybody says that is Free Enterprise in action, that is not Free Enterprise in action; that is anarchy in action, and that is corruption in action, and it has nothing to do with Free Enterprise. It is like turning your kid loose with a loaded gun—it is the same thing—and saying, "Do your own thing . If you shoot somebody, tough." In my opinion, it is no better or no worse.

I'll give you an example of the military and drugs. If they really decided to stop it—and this is what Bob's talking about, and he is a hundred percent right—and they went in for random testing and random searching with the dogs and everything right out here at Lackland and the other bases, I guarantee you they would cut down on the use of drugs dramatically.

You ask why should they have to do that. I tell you that these kids are nothing more or less than the society from which they come. But things have changed. They have changed because, one, it is not acceptable everywhere, and two, there are strong, stringent regulations to do something about it.

As long as our society finds it even marginally acceptable, as long as peer level areas find it acceptable, it is going to be a problem. When we finally decide that it is not acceptable and we are not going to put up with it, then we will start to get rid of the drug problem. When you look at countries where twenty-five or maybe thirty percent of their entire national economy is based upon drugs, as Bob talks about, you are going to have the pressure of "push." What you are going to have to do is cut out the vacuum. If you cut out the vacuum like Japan did, where they have a death penalty for pushing, you make it strong enough, and I will guarantee you, you will make it to the point where people won't want to do it.

Now, as long as the people read in the paper that fifteen percent or ten percent of the executives in this country are sniffing cocaine and that type of thing, it is going to be a problem. You have got to get just as tough with secretaries as with the Presidents of the companies. It is just not acceptable for anybody. Until you reach that point, you are not going to solve the problem.

Abuses in the Market System

Sidney Greenburg:

I would like to follow that up a little bit here. Whatever else we say, we still come back to the question: What do you do about the confusion between the wrong use of capitalism and Free Enterprise and its legitimate use?

Let me give you an example; Liberation Theology. As the previous speaker mentioned; he said it is Marxism, it is socialism. How do we convince the liberal theologians of the error of their ways and of the misconceptions they are suffering through which the majority is so misled. The reason we are given for going into the Sandanista situation is because of the abuses of the capitalistic society.

That is the interpretation there. Are we sure that we have made the necessary distinctions in the United States? We must not have, or we would not be confused.

What has happened here? Where is the education system that demonstrates that the people in this country understand responsible Free Enterprise, the capitalistic system? Where is the incentive to teach the philosophy of freedom and Free Enterprise? Where other than St. Mary's University whose faculty is one of the few in the entire country who does research and teaches the essentials of this philosophy?

As I see it, we cannot talk about "our people" and "their people."

They will tell you that the reason they are acting that way is because of the misery that misguided capitalism has caused down there. That is the first paragraph of the Manifesto of the Communist party, where it states that all values are distorted, where it says that all problems, hunger and poverty and so forth, are based upon an economic system that must be broken and changed. That is why they say change the infrastructure, and you will change the values. They say change the capitalistic values, and you will change society.

That is a problem to worry about which to me is much more important that the drug problem, because the drug problem is an effect of the kind of reasoning that we have done. I would like to know what we are going to do other than what we are doing here at St. Mary's. We have a bigger problem in this country than I think many of us have any idea of.

Robert West:

Sidney, I would like to comment that I hope that this is not right. I hope that there is not a feeling in this country or around the world that the system of Free Enterprise connotes ultimate freedom to do anything you want; that it connotes the total lack of discipline, that it connotes the total lack of ethics or morality, and values of that kind.

I used the word "discipline" earlier in my comments, and evidently I did not go far enough in that. I would say, first of all, there is nothing free that I know of in life. And perhaps the phrase "Free Enterprise," even though it is one that we use quite often to describe the economic system which we enjoy, maybe is not a broad enough or a descriptive enough term. It really needs some qualifications or descriptive adjectives. The phrase "Free Enterprise" should not be interpreted as meaning a system with absolutely no restraints on it.

I would go beyond that and say that looking at the title of this Symposium, "Moral Wisdom in the Allocation of Economic Resources," I would suggest that that is the essence of the Free

Enterprise system. I would suggest that there are other factors included in the phrase "economic resources" than just money or goods or dollar equivalents; this is particularly true for a corporation, which is the point of view which I can express. It is also true for a governmental entity.

Among some of these other economic resources are what you can call other than balance sheet assets. Some of those other resources are values as integrity, truth, honesty, compassion, leadership, social awareness, social understanding, good will toward others, respect for the rights of others, and group discipline, and you could go on and on.

But those things to me are implicit in the exercise of the process that we call Free Enterprise. Just as Louis said a minute ago, and I think he made a very good point, that almost every corporate executive that I know of is required every year, particularly if he is in a public corporation, which Louis and I are involved in, to sign an affidavit that he has complied with the law, with the ethics of Private Enterprise, that he has not bribed anybody, or getting anything for his company by illicit means.

All of those things need to be understood by people outside this room, and I am talking about the whole country and the whole world, but they are not, unfortunately. So I come back to my first statement, that the phrase "Free Enterprise" connotes a lot more than just total freedom to do whatever you want to do, whenever, under any of the circumstances that present themselves, that would lead to your own economic gain.

Confusion of Economic Philosophy

Sidney Greenburg:

You said there is a confusion there. I am glad you said that. Confusion is encountered in important areas. Again we come back to the initial question asked here, and this is something that we tend to take for granted. I do not think we should take anything for granted in the educational system and the society in which we live.

For example, the Economic Pastoral by the Bishops in its final form: that document contains many sections and paragraphs that you can pick out and identify as contributing to the confusion, as the injudicious use of the term capitalism. The authors imply that the opposite of Marxist socialism is perverted capitalism. Very little is said on behalf of those who tried to say, "No, no, unbridled materialism is not capitalism; that is not Free Enterprise; that is a pejorative misuse of the term." But you do not find it in that document.

I want to pose the question again, as it came from the gentleman from Miami, for our general discussion. The Miami example is not the crux but just one example of the misuse of some of the characteristics of the philosophy of Free Enterprise with which basically all of us identify. How do we stop its misuse?

Erik von Kuehnelt-Leddihn:

I think that this question is very much deeper. I published this summer an article entitled "If There Is No God," and I terminated it by quoting Dostoevski: "If there is no God, everything is permitted." In other words, we have to come down to religion. I think about Oliver Wendell Holmes, who told us the ideal murder is a purely illogical notion, that there is something bad about it. Unfortunately we are not all agreed in our thinking.

The question here really relates to values. Liberalism, rightly understood, which has nothing to do with democracy, says human beings should have the full right to do everything provided it is compatible with the common good. Of course, the common good complicates the picture, where we see the other end where people are drifting without fixed values. Fixed values we only get from God's revealed word, not from human constructions. In other words, we have merely to return to the Bible.

We see that in a number of state universities there are gay clubs, and these gay clubs are financed by the state university, and that means the government finances the spread of homosexuality in this country.

This drifting without values is really permissiveness. I do not think that problem has anything really to do with Free Enterprise. We have gotten far afield in discussing it, but I could not resist pointing out some things that I personally find disgusting.

Louis Stumberg:

Doctor, you mentioned universities. Like Dr. West, I am on the board of a church-related university. I am on the board of Trinity University. I have long contended, I strongly contend, that a church-related university has a higher standard to meet than does a public university. We have a higher responsibility that parents can expect of us, and it is our job to produce. We have a higher moral standard than a public university.

Defining that standard is sometimes very difficult, particularly when you get into academic freedom and everything else. But, Doctor, I would suggest to you that professors or priests within a church-related university should understand that they have a different standard than in a public university. It is the nature of the institution. It is one of the great things of this country that we can have both.

Now, in line with what you said, we can teach values within a church-related university, but it is very difficult for a public university to do so. That is one of our great strengths, that we can teach values, and we should teach values; there is an absolute obligation upon us to do so.

Labor and Welfare

Question: First, I would just like to comment on the term "Free Enterprise" before I ask my question. I have always used "Private Enterprise," and I think it is far more explanatory of what we are really talking about, so that nobody can be confused.

I would like to ask either gentleman how we can curtail the demand for this cradle-to-the-grave mentality that labor has pushed onto industry?

Robert West:

The question is how we can curtail the cradle-to-the-grave mentality that labor has pushed onto industry. I think it is already being curtailed by its own processes. If you look at union membership throughout the country, the various unions now are not even close to what they were fifty years ago.

I happened to see an article in *The Wall Street Journal* the other day that specifically related to the United Mine Workers and shows their membership peaked back in 1936 during the heyday of John L. Lewis and also during the heyday of the coal industry. The semi-demise of the coal industry has had something to do with, but that is not the key factor; rather an attendant change on the part of the work force was influential.

If I remember the membership figures correctly, the membership of the UMW has gone from a peak of about seven hundred thousand in 1936 to slightly less than maybe a hundred thousand, maybe seventy-some-odd thousand, in 1986, in a period of fifty years. That is a drastic drop in a sort of a militant union activity that we cannot say has taken place throughout our entire economy, but I would suggest to you that to a certain extent it has, that people are beginning to lose that cradle-to-the-grave mentality.

Part of it is because of the change in our industrial structure. This is a negative, in my judgment, the loss of our industrial infrastructure to other countries; and the competitive economic forces at work in other countries under which people in Japan, for instance, or in Korea or Taiwan or Hong Kong or wherever, are willing to work for less. Japan, I guess, is the most vivid example of a people who are willing to work for less and produce fine products.

So the competitive forces of the world are gradually changing this mentality. I do not perceive unions as being nearly as strong now as they were when I was a young man.

Question: Excuse me, I realize that, but, for example,
                   our police, our firemen do not reflect that
                   trend; and, as you speak about Japan, there
                   is a new Japanese plant in Tennessee, and
                   the unions are trying to force unionism on
                   them. The cradle-to-the-grave mentality is
                   still a definite problem that prevails in this
                   country.

Robert West:

Well, there is probably a natural attitude of people who feel
somewhat impotent in dealing with the circumstances of life that
they have to deal with, and so they—and we all do this in one way
or another—group together to detract from their impotency.

That is one explanation. I do not think you will ever get away
from that. But I do see a lessening in this cradle-to-the-grave type
of socialistic attitude, that you have to take care of me whether I
work or not.

The Golden Parachute

Question: Does not the "golden parachute" for the
                   administrators reflect the cradle-to-the-grave
                   kind of thinking charge? That is a charge
                   that always seems to be leveled at labor, but
                   it seems that feeling exists in a lot of areas
                   and relates more to a sense of security; we
                   seem to live in a very insecure situation. I
                   would just like your comment on the
                   "golden parachute."

Robert West:

There are limitations by law to three times annual salary for
executives. That is a much shorter timeframe and is not quite the
same as the old cradle-to-the-grave concept. Although it is a
shorter timeframe, I suppose when you think of it from the standpoint of economic security, you can translate that into something

similar to the economic security to people on the labor side as opposed to people on the management side.

Third World Development

Louis Stumberg:

You have a valid point. Management is in many cases as guilty as the union in seeking economic security. Up until a few years ago – and Dr. West put his finger on it – if costs went up, you raised your prices. You did not have to be more efficient. You could grant any wage increase.

What has happened in the last five years is that the picture has changed, and we now compete with the world and not on a level playing field. Now, that would take another whole symposium, and I would love sometime to tell you about some of the playing field levels that exist for us and that exist within the other nation itself, whether it be Japan or any other nation. It is not a level playing field; that condition is putting enormous pressure on our own people.

It is the first time in my history of forty years of being in business that I realize that the multinational corporation has developed a concept of manufacturing, there is the recognition, that you can use the same technology and the same machinery in other countries as you can in this country; and, therefore, you manufacture wherever it is cheapest.

Twenty years ago Americans could come up with a great idea, and it would be hatched, raised, and produced in this country. Not anymore.

If you have read *The Wall Street Journal* in the last few days, you know that one of the major companies had planned the most innovative automobile plant in the world. It was to be all American. What are they talking about today? They are now talking about offshore production, if you will, to produce some of those parts.

That is one of the conditions that now exists; the manufacturing can be done in Japan, Taiwan, Korea, and elsewhere.

Depreciating the dollar is not really the answer to it; it is a partial answer. Depreciating the dollar only affects fifty percent of imports brought into this country. The other fifty percent is in nations where their currency is in one way or another tied to our currency. If our currency has gone down, their currency has gone down. But this is such an important subject that if we took a whole day or a week or a month, it could stand on its own.

Sidney Greenburg:

I want to comment on that before we get away from it. Louis touched on something of great importance not necessarily to my generation but to the generations that are coming ahead. It is not just important but it has fantastic significance. It is that the economy, call it the Private Enterprise system, if you will, or the Free Enterprise system, the economy is changing dramatically and it is really becoming worldwide with instantaneous communications, given very short-term travel capabilities; and the transfer of technology is widespread.

Louis commented earlier about China. I have been there. Just wait until the Chinese really get in the act of competitive production of goods, which they certainly will do in the not too distant future. They will make the Japanese look as impotent and helpless as the Japanese have made us look, and then India is going to be passing everybody by.

In my judgment, unless some dramatic changes come about, we will see a tremendous lowering in our standard of living in the western world as a result of the ability and willingness of people in what we call the Third World now to take jobs and to produce goods at a much lower wage rate than we in this country and the rest of the western world envision.

Defining Our Terms

Sidney Greenburg:

Before I ask for any other questions, I cannot resist as a philosopher saying in response to the person who spoke of our changing our terminology from "Free" to "Private," that you are jumping from a fundamental freedom for which both the public and the private sectors are responsible. Both the public and the private sectors have to be free first, and that is what we have to consider first, "freedom." "Private Enterprise" means in the hands of private individuals vis-a-vis in the hands of public individuals or the state. That still does not tell us what Free Enterprise and the philosophy of freedom is all about.

Responsibility to the Third World

Question: Basically, with respect to the topic of today's conversation, "Moral Wisdom in the Allocation of Economic Resources," Dr. von Kuehnelt-Leddihn discussed the fact that he thought that our responsibility does not lie in assisting the Third World, that it lies in our responsibility for ourselves. I must say that I concur with him.

However, we still have the Third World. We have been assisting the Third World monetarily at great expense to ourselves, and more importantly and more closely Central America and even Mexico.

I would like to ask the panelists what their consideration is versus the Doctor's consideration as to what is our responsibility and what is the appropriate moral wisdom in the allocation of our economic resources relative to the Third World?

Sidney Greenburg:

Before we discuss that, in anticipation of what you may say, may I interpret you, sir, in what you said? I think there is some slight confusion here about what you actually meant. I thought that you said that you were concentrating on the responsibility of the "us" first rather than to "them." I think you were implying that the responsibility to ourselves leads to the correct responsibility with respect to others and the common good; whereas if you reverse the situation, the responsibility to the former would lead to the responsibility to ourselves. thus, there is no fundamental difference. That is what I thought you were talking about.

Erik von Kuehnelt-Leddihn:
   That is right.
   I do think that we have a duty of charity toward the Third World, yes; contributions, no. You must never forget that the Washington/Moscow axis – I can be more of a beneficist than you are – has resulted in the creation of the Third World in Africa and a great part of Asia. These adopted children are now in their early puberty and have run away from their parental home and, of course, have accused us of lacking interest; the European countries paid through the nose for these ex-colonies.
   Now the question is how will we materially aid them. I think of a CCC program in your country a few years ago. We were confronted by a gentleman who said: "For heaven's sake, do not support us financially. We will never ever learn to stand on our own feet."
   Dollar aid increases corruption in those countries tremendously. There is a whole European literature on that subject, even by European socialists, by people coming from the left. Our policies in respect to the Third World really are among the handouts. I understand that there are earthquakes, floods, emergency situations, hunger, which are extended, of course, by Communist regimes; which in the old days were managed by colonial powers.
   My country never had colonies but backed colonialism up to the hilt, and I think in America those who attack colonialism should get good medical attention because it was through British colonialism we have the United States of America; and of your own country you must be proud.

Robert West:

I do not think there is any easy answer to the question, which fundamentally is: Should the United States be obligated to help Third World countries?

I do not think we are obligated other than in terms of human concepts and maybe our own self-interest. I think that is a big "maybe." I think we are obligated to help ourselves first. From a Christian standpoint, we are obligated to help people in dire need, which is a different situation.

Third World Population

Robert West:

I would like to bring up a subject that is a very touchy one, particularly in the environmental setting in which we are today, but I would say to you that I feel strongly that the world cannot support the runaway population growth which it is experiencing, and I think that is one of the fundamental problems that exists economically, socially, politically, everywhere you can think of. Some countries have an almost exponential rate.

Perhaps Louis could comment on his experience in China last year. China has set an example in controlling the population rate and at the same time permitting her citizens to begin to exercise the principles of Free Enterprise.

Take Latin America. Take Mexico. The population growth in Mexico without the attendant expansion in the economy of Mexico and without the attendant expansion in the economies of Latin American nations is critical. This is a problem that will not go away, and the world is facing a very, very, very explosive situation; and the drug situation in Miami is just one little manifestation of it.

Those people, a lot of them, have no other way to make money except by what amounts to an illicit imposition on and infringement of American rights, our human rights, as well as the rights of others. Maybe they are dumb customers of drugs and do not want to work, but that is an imposition on the human rights of others.

Recently I flew from southern Bolivia and up over northeastern Bolivia and over the Amazon Valley for literally thousands of miles. We saw nothing whatsoever in the valley under cultivation. But the flight over northeastern Bolivia was where our troops have been trying to operate to stamp out cocaine raising, and the interesting thing was that you saw these little isolated air strips, you could see them everywhere, every twenty to thirty miles. They were all over, and if they were in one location, they would be one big airpark. But you could not see any farm houses; you could not see any what you would consider in this country, ranches or cattle raising operations or anything like that. But you saw the air strips and no houses. I guess they raise the coke under the trees; you could not see it from the air. It is a very low level economic activity. These people are willing to work for nothing because the population is expanding, and they have no other sources of supporting themselves.

We, people who are halfway intelligent and hopefully more than halfway concerned, have to do something about the exploding world population because we are not going to have a chance if we do not.

Louis Stumberg:

If there was not another baby born in Mexico, the problem would exist for the next eighteen years in the need for jobs in a country that before the oil crisis had a forty percent unemployment or underemployment rate. What it is today nobody knows.

When you ask what is our obligation, what can we do? Open borders? We very nearly have that right now. No nation in the world can long exist with the open borders that we have. I do not take the responsibility for the troubles that exist in Mexico, period. They try to foist them on us. They say, "That is your responsibility." I will not accept that. That is their responsibility, and I will help them with it; but it is not my responsibility, and I am absolutely adamant on that particular position.

One final comment. Bad as we say things are, this nation, since

World War II, has given more money than all the rest of the world combined in the history of mankind. Did you know that?

Now, what are we expected to do when we are running a huge deficit as we are?

Finally, I suggest that anybody that complains and talks about this country, look at which way the footprints in the sand and in the dust are headed. They are not headed south of our borders; they are headed to our borders. That is our problem. Now we have already done more than all of the rest of the world combined. What more can we do? I don't know, but I am not going to say that I am taking the burden of the world on today when we are having as much difficulty as we are in wrestling with our own economy.

CONCLUSION

Sidney Greenburg:

In concluding this Forum part of our Symposium I would like to make this comment on the philosophy of Free Enterprise. In doing that I go back to the Founding Fathers. I think of our Founding Fathers when the American Revolution was over and they had just won their freedom; they are sitting around the table, and a big question comes up: "Now that we have just won our freedom what are we going to do with it?"

As they talk about that, the biggest question of all arises: "How are we going to implement our newly won freedom; politically, socially, and economically?"

Actually they did a pretty good job. Our Founding Fathers chose a political system of democracy, and economically they chose a free market, a philosophy of Free Enterprise; and they set the stage Constitutionally for defining what our Republic needed to be.

Thank you very much.

RICHARD JOHN NEUHAUS

RICHARD JOHN NEUHAUS

Richard John Neuhaus graces the podium of many cultural groups, organizations, and universities in cities across the country.

Born in Pembroke, Ontario, Canada, Pastor Neuhaus was educated in Ontario, Nebraska, and Texas. He studied theology at Concordia Theological Seminary in St. Louis, and philosophy and sociology at Washington University in St. Louis, and Wayne State University in Detroit.

A Lutheran clergyman, he served pastoral internships in Detroit and Chicago. For seventeen years he was Senior Pastor of a low-income Black and Hispanic parish in Brooklyn, New York. Over the years he has played a leadership role in numerous organizations dealing with civil rights, peace, international justice, and religious ecumenism.

His work and writing have been the subject of feature articles in *TIME*, *NEWSWEEK*, *THE NEW YORK TIMES MAGAZINE*, and scholarly publications. In 1982 he received the "Faith and Freedom Award" from the Religious Heritage Foundation of America and in 1983 the John Paul II "Award for Religious Freedom."

For eight years he was Senior Editor of *Worldview*, a monthly journal on ethics and social change. Also, he served as project director at the Council on Religion and International Affairs, an Andrew Carnegie foundation in New York City. He serves on the boards and editorial councils of a number of organizations dealing with theology and public affairs, and is the editor of *Lutheran Forum Letter*. In addition, he is a member of an international research project, SABA (South Africa Beyond Apartheid). Since 1984 Pastor Neuhaus has been the Director of The Center on Religion and Society, New York City, and the editor of *The Religion and Society Report*.

The range of Pastor Neuhaus' perspective is revealed through his scholarly writings. His books include: *Theology and the Kingdom of God* (1969), analyzing the theology of Wolfhart Pannenberg; *Movement and Revolution* (with Peter Berger, 1970), a study on the nature of revolution in American and other societies; *In Defense of People* (1971), the first book-length critique of environmentalism as it relates to ideas of social justice; *Against the World for the World* (edited, 1976), the debate over the Hartford Appeal of 1975 and its meaning for the churches; *Time Toward Home — The American Experiment as Revelation* (1975), a critically acclaimed study of the nature of American democracy; *Christian Faith and Public Policy* (1977), a detailed analysis of connections between Christian faith and public policy-making; *To Empower People* (with Peter Berger, 1977), on the role of "mediating structures" (family, church, etc.) in public policy; *Freedom For Ministry* (1979), a critical affirmation of the theory and practice of Christian ministry; *The Naked Public Square* (1984), an analysis of public policy and public life in "post-secular" America; and *Dispensations* (1986), on the role of religion in the future of South Africa, as viewed by South Africans.

Contemporary culture and that of the future is indebted to Pastor Neuhaus for advancing the humanitarian ethos theologically, philosophically, and with elegance.

ETHICS AND ECONOMICS

Richard John Neuhaus

THE RELATION BETWEEN ETHICS AND ECONOMICS

The subject I have been assigned is "Ethics and Economics." Let me say right at the beginning that there are a good many people, a good many thoughtful people, who think the subject itself is illegitimate, that it is oxymoronic, that there is a contradiction in terms here. Of course, I speak primarily about our gullible libertarian friends, who would persuade us, at least some of them would, that any discussion of ethics and economics is illegitimate. Any moral, ethical reflection of intervention in the free market process can only confuse and distort and lead to unhappy consequences for everybody concerned except, of course, for the government officials and architects who design and administer the interventions.

Well, I am not a libertarian. I have great respect for some libertarian arguments. I have some good friends who are libertarians. One of them is such a conscientious and consistent libertarian that he claims he deeply resents the Invisible Hand.

Actually, he is a person who tries to be morally and theologically reflective, although at times there are debates in which we find ourselves, and in which we will continue to find ourselves, in this confused realm of ethics and economics.

I have arrived at a position that is very deeply committed to liberal democracy. I am deeply committed to the fact that there seems to be a connection between liberal democracy and market economics, and that connection impresses me deeply. In coming to that conclusion and commitment, I find myself, of course, in rather sharp disagreement with people who believe that a weight of moral judgment is, after all is said and done, *against* market economics and *for* something that, in one version or another, is socialism, whether called democratic socialism or social democracy or whatever.

I have a friend at Harvard, who also is an economist, who said that for years and years he was a very deeply devoted socialist, and he studied socialism, and he talked socialism, and he ate and he slept socialism, and he read everything there was to read about socialism until he arrived at the point at which he understood socialism backwards and forwards and inside and out. He said that at that point he became a capitalist. The reason is very simple, and that is he could never respect an economic system that he could understand.

There is a certain wisdom in that.

If you are going to talk about ethics and economics, we are assuming that there is a link, a legitimate link, a necessary link, between moral reflection and the public disclosure associated with it on the one hand, and our economic behavior and decision-making, on the other—I believe there is such a link. In this sense I agree with my friend Michael Novak that when we are talking about democratic capitalism we are not speaking, first of all, certainly not exclusively, about economics. We are speaking rather about the political economy. We are speaking about the role of economics within a much more comprehensive matrix of ideas, attitudes, behavioral patterns, moral judgments, and that is where it seems to me we have located the title of my remarks, "Ethics and

Economics."

I have to say that I come to this question and have come to it over the years, as all of us do, with a very clear bias, with a developing bias and a changing bias, and I trust, an informed bias. My own bias on the questions of economics and what is called economic justice has been very much shaped by my years as pastor in the Williamsburg/ Bedford-Stuyvesant section of Brooklyn among the poorest of what is called the urban black underclass of America. When I think of these questions, and listen to economists and others speak about these questions, I can visualize in my mind's eye and in my ear that I am watching and listening and understanding through that experience of Williamsburg/ Bedford-Stuyvesant in Brooklyn, always asking myself the question – and this is not the only question but an important question – what does that mean, what this person is saying, for the special grant that he proposes? What does that mean for the well-being of the people of Bedford-Stuyvesant?

PREFERENTIAL OPTION FOR THE POOR

In that sense, there is, I think, a legitimacy to the phrase that has gained such great currency in recent years – preferential option for the poor. We ought always to be looking for how any idea, program, proposal, policy that can help those who are on the margins, those who live at the fault lines rather than the success lines of a society.

And it seems to me one of the sad things in recent years, although it really is not that recent – it really goes back to the debate of these questions over the last two hundred years – the sad thing that those who profess to be concerned for the poor, that those who talk most persistently and frequently persuasively about compassion, are the ones who succeed in setting themselves against democratic capitalism and the market economies that accompany, perhaps necessarily accompany, free societies.

We who understand the extraordinary achievement of a free society, we who understand that the American experiment in particular is as audacious an idea and as continually an experiment as it was two hundred years ago, we who understand those truths must never, never, never let those who do not understand those truths pass themselves off as the partisans of the poor or as people who have a monopoly on the implications of what it means to explore a preferential option for the poor.

THE EVOLUTION OF PHILOSOPHICAL THOUGHT

In my own history in the shaping of my own bias, I have moved from a position that in the 1960's was perceived as being left, liberal, even radical to a position that in the last ten years is frequently described as being neither conservative nor liberal. Most of this, I think, has to do less with Richard John Neuhaus that it has to do with the shifting course of dialogues and debates and labels in our society.

This is not to say for a moment that I have not changed. I have changed in thinking about these questions. Indeed, I have been inspired over the years by John Henry Cardinal Newman's observation that to live is to change and to be good is to have changed often, so I am manifestly on my way to perfection.

But there are some things which have guided me, I think, in a very clear continuum in my thinking about questions of ethics, polity, and economic justice. I think I have been or tried to be over the years a person who is theologically orthodox, who is culturally conservative, who is politically liberal, again in the historic sense of that word, and who is economically skeptical or pragmatic, and that is the bias which I unabashedly present to you.

I believe that the economic question is not the most important question, emphatically not the most important question. Now, those who would make it the most important question, whether they be liberation theologians of a Marxist propensity or extreme libertarians at the other end of the spectrum, or both, I believe, are making a very grievous error.

In a curious kind of way there is a queer Marxism operative among some of our friends on the right, who believe that finally the question, the phenomenon to which everything else is epi-phenomenal, is economics. It is a very strange thing, how many who consider themselves conservative divide into what is in principle subscribed to by the greatest enemy of western civilization and the free society. They have subscribed to this notion that somehow you begin with religious and moral questions and then you move from there to the philosophical questions and then, as you get more serious, you move to the political questions, and then when you really hit bedrock, you move to the economic questions.

That, I think, is utter nonsense. In my judgment, that is to get things exactly backwards. The economic questions, rather, lead to the political questions and then to the philosophical questions and then to the moral questions and then to the theological questions. Finally, at least in my own thinking and in the thinking of those by whom I have been most deeply influenced and for whom I have the deepest respect, that has been the trajectory, if you will, of thought.

THE LOSS OF THEOLOGICAL GUIDELINES

It is a particularly sordid thing that very many of our churches today, not only in the Roman Catholic Church by any means, but among the Anglicans, which thought was molded by American Catholicism, and among the social-gospel-oriented Protestantism people, have bought into the reverse part of that trajectory of thought. I think people often buy into it without knowing what they have done.

Some years ago, about three or four, I was speaking to a large group of five or six hundred Roman Catholic clergy in the upper Midwest, and the bishop who introduced me said to his clergy: "Now, we have been here for two days, and we have been discussing liturgy and sacramental theology, which is, of course, all very important; but now we have Pastor Neuhaus with us, and he is going to return us to the real world on the subject of religion and politics." The real world?

Now, I do not think for a minute that that bishop really meant what his statement clearly implies, but it was a slip of tongue that reveals a slip of mind. It is characteristic of American religious leadership today across the board to believe that somehow the mission of the Church is being most centrally advanced and the great questions of our time most significantly engaged when we address ourselves to the questions that the front page of the *New York Times* says are the most important questions of our times.

In short, we have lost our theological barriers, and this is much deeper, the source of the problem, than anything one may agree with or disagree with in the latest pronunciamento, et cetera coming down from the United Methodist Bishops' Council or from the Roman Catholic Bishops' meeting in Washington during which they will approve the Final Draft of the Pastoral Letter on Catholic Social Teaching and the U. S. Economy. Much more important than anything they said about the merits or demerits of this economic policy or that economic policy; much more important are the presuppositions about the nature of the Church, the nature of the Faith, the nature of history and of the Christian role within history. It is often what is between the lines, the taken-for-granted assumptions, that need most sharply be examined.

For I believe that politics is largely a function of culture, and at the heart of culture is religion. And by "religion" here I do not mean any brand-name religion, Christianity, Judaism, whatever; but rather religion in the root sense of the word, "religious," that which binds people together, the most binding beliefs, the ultimate beliefs by which people live or think they should live: politics, culture, religion.

In the political sphere we can only do those things and advance those programs which the culture makes possible; namely, the prevailing ideas, the pervasive habits of mind or behavior, the understanding or lack of understanding with respect to the meaning of virtue and vice. These are the things that your culture either provides or it does not provide, and either transmits or fails to transmit; which determines, of course, what can be done politically, and therefore, what can be done economically. It does not seem to me that the idea of a political economy, such as the Founders of this audacious American experiment crafted, is one in which there is not a keen appreciation of both the viciousness of human behavior and how it must be checked; but also of the necessity of virtue in human behavior and how virtue could be channeled and encouraged and also protected.

Economics in almost every instance is the consequence of what happens in the political decisions about economic behavior, which, in turn, is determined by the culture, which, in turn, is determined by those beliefs, religion, that people hold to be most important and binding.

DEMOCRATIC CAPITALISM

Standing significantly, one little thing, about the founding notion that impresses me deeply, is that in the Constitution itself, aside from the Bill of Rights, the word "right" only occurs once, and that is in the first Article, a commercial one. The right to patent and to benefit from invention: the Founders understood not only that these potentialities were there and necessary to the economic well-being of society, but also that there had to be the political provision to make sure that they were protected, that they were not destroyed.

I am not, not even as much as my friend Michael Novak, a God-fearing promoter of democratic capitalism as such; I trust it is evident from the structure of my argument today. It is rather, that my commitment to democratic capitalism is a consequence of prior commitments: theological, religious, political, cultural.

I am impressed by three propositions, one which is a theological proposition and the other two which are simply empirical observations.

The theological proposition is this: that in any society, anywhere, anytime, the greatest good, the greatest social good, is what we call religious freedom or freedom of conscience; namely, the institutional acknowledgment that every person is an absolute point, if you will, in the encounter with transcendent truth and that that encounter, however it may be expressed, whether in orthodox religion or in some other way, must be institutionally respected. This, I believe, is the source of all other notions of human rights and of human dignity, and it is always under attack, even in our society. That is the theological proposition with respect to the highest social good.

Then comes the empirical observation. That is, that if one looks around the world today at the hundred and sixty nations that belong to the United Nations, many of which are nations primarily because they belong to the United Nations; but be that as it may, if you look at the nations of the world, the only place where religious freedom or freedom of conscience is reasonably guaranteed by institutional protection are those societies that are, or aspire to be, liberal democracies, without exception.

That does not mean that liberal democracy is the necessary causal condition without which religious rights and human rights and civil and political liberties cannot exist. Obviously in history we can find all of these and all kinds of arrangements in which there was religious freedom.

But today in the world nowhere, I would suggest, does it exist other than in those societies that are or aspire to become liberal democratic societies.

And the third proposition, again an empirical observation, is that nowhere in the world today do you find liberal democracies or republic governments, in whatever form they might be; nowhere do you find them, except in those societies which have a predominant market economy.

Now, that does not mean that a market economy is a sine qua non for democracy and for religious freedom. That would be a hard argument to make logically; but empirically, in terms of the historical evidence, no sane person can fail to be impressed by the coincidence of these three, which it is reasonable to believe is more than simply a mere coincidence.

It is very difficult for many in our churches, in our laboratories, in our universities, and in our media to appreciate the kind of argument which I am attempting to advance. You see every day the lack of appreciation of it, often because of the people who have a deep hostility against poverty problems, a hostility that is the product of what they believe to be a deep compassion and concern for those who they perceive are injured by market economics. Certainly this is true within our society, and there are many difficult issues within our society, but much more true when you leave our society and enter into debates in the so-called Third World.

THE POLITICAL POWER OF THE SOCIALIST ARGUMENT

It is going to be exceedingly difficult to make the argument for human dignity, democracy, and market economics in the years ahead, just as it has been exceedingly difficult in the decade just past. One reason for this is that those on the other side, whether or not they call themselves socialists, democratic socialists, liberal socialists, social democrats, whatever—those on the other side have such a deep investment in the network of political power of the socialist argument.

Irving Howe, one of the few major American intellectuals who is still candid enough to call himself a socialist publicly, a very intelligent person, writes in *Dissent* magazine that: "Of course, we recognize, we socialists, the evidence of recent years that, in fact, there is no social democratic society or experiment in the world to which we can point that is both truly socialist and truly democratic." And he says: "If you were simply working on the basis of historical evidence, you would have to stop being a socialist"; but, he says, "we are not subject to such reaction as reasonable." "Socialism," he says, "is the name of our game, our inspiration, our dream."

How do you go up against a powerful dream, a vision of religious effect in the lives and in the minds of many, many Americans and millions upon millions of intellectual writers and church people around the world?

It is a difficult thing to do because a dream is not subject to empirical classification.

I would have to take a perhaps slight exception to some comments which were said earlier this morning in the part I was able to participate in with regard to Peter Berger's new book, called *The Capitalist Revolution*. Some of you are familiar with it, I am sure. It has been out about six weeks now. It is subtitled "Fifty Propositions about Prosperity, Equality, and Liberty."

The strength of the book, which I think is one of the most important books to appear in many years on the question of ethics and economics, the strength of Peter Berger's *The Capitalist Revolution* is precisely that he subjects all the arguments and counterarguments that have been made in the socialist/capitalist debate to empirical scrutiny of the most painful kind. He sets forth his admittedly pro democratic capitalistic argument in a manner that is with almost painful honesty, quite hypothetical.

He says, "Let us hypothesize that such-and-such may be the case, that there may be a connection between certain cultural virtues and economic productivity; that those societies, let us hypothesize, that accept liberty, in fact, do better by both liberty and equality than do those societies that accept equality." And so he goes on and on with his fifty hypotheses. Yet, in making his case, which I think is not only persuasive but convincing—as I say, one of the most important books in many years, in my judgment, treating of moral judgments and economic decisions—we have to realize it will be of limited effectiveness because those for whom socialism is the name of their dream will never permit themselves to be vulnerable to the empirical test.

Whatever you can say about socialism in the world—Vietnamese, Soviet, Chinese, any at all—they really believe. But that is not the socialism that I am talking about. My socialism has not been tried yet. My socialism flies on gossamer wings above the sleazy particularities of the historical event, and it cannot be touched by your scientific critiques.

THE FAILURE OF THE MIDDLE WAY

That, I am afraid, ladies and gentlemen, is one of the problems we have had for a very long time and are going to continue to have. The answer to it is not, I think, to demonstrate that capitalism, democratic capitalism, can construct a middle way to generate a vision of equal power with socialism.

In a sense, it cannot. It cannot precisely for all the reasons that I alluded to earlier, namely because we do not believe, as the opposition does, that economics is really the heart of things. We believe there are higher truths about human nature and about history and about the purpose of life, and about the Church, and our God, and about the transcendent immortality within time. And, therefore, we can never lift up any economic system and put it on a pedestal almost to the point of idolatry that our socialist opponents can and do.

We cannot, even in a surfeit of success of democratic capitalism wherever it has been tried around the world, wherever economic and cultural conditions have been sympathetic to it. More and more people are aware of that success and are seeing that it is not limited to the American or to the Western, Asian, European, or whatever experiment. We have seen its success in Japan and seen it in Singapore, we have seen it in Taiwan and many other places in the world, even in Africa, where you can test your ideas as far as the Ivory Coast, where they have been at least somewhat more sympathetic to the way we handle our market economies as against what they have had in contrast.

DEMOCRATIC CAPITALISM AND THE POOR

Democratic capitalism wins, and wins precisely for the poor. It wins precisely because part of the historical and preferential option is for the poor. It is a lot better for the poor, instead of being given alms, to participate in the mainstream of economic productivity and achievement.

I know, coming back to my opening, as far as the people of

Williamsburg/Bedford-Stuyvesant in the Brooklyn section of New York are concerned, that the vision that should win is a vision that takes the ways in which a majority of black Americans in the last twenty years have been able to participate in the mainstream of economic achievement. We have to ask ourselves: How now can that achievement be extended? How can we adopt policies which will stop preventing its extension to the so-called black underclass?

Our problem from our side of the picture is not to build walls beyond policies, beyond the societies that are in deep trouble — there are sections of society that are in deep trouble. But, rather, to look to the strong points and see how can we build permanently along the strong points, where enterprise and entrepreneurship, and vision and work, with delayed gratification and work, where all these things can be capitalized upon, precisely for the sake of the poor.

In doing that we have made some little headway in recent years with the social and political and cultural changes that are taking place in our society. But I say to you: We are still way behind because we do not lift up democratic capitalism as the means of the salvation of mankind. We do not say of democratic capitalism that it is a name for our dream. It is the name, rather, of our duty, of our duty to continue to make the arguments about the linkage between economics, religion, morality, politics, and economic freedom, and not only to make that argument but also to encourage all of our sisters and brothers and including most especially the poor among us to demonstrate the effectiveness of that argument.

That is a huge task. It is a task for all the rest of our lives and for generations to come, a part of this audacious American experiment.

DOUGLAS J. CULVER

DOUGLAS J. CULVER

Douglas J. Culver is an ordained minister serving as Senior Minister of Granada Presbyterian Church in Coral Gables, Florida. He holds the Ph.D. in Hebraics and Near East Studies from New York University; the Th.M. in Systematic Theology (Magna Cum Laude) from Trinity Evangelical Divinity School, Deerfield, Illinois; the M.Div. in Old Testament (Summa Cum Laude) from Bethel Theological Seminary, St. Paul, Minnesota; and the B.A. in Social Science from Wheaton College, Wheaton, Illinois. He has done additional post graduate work in Hebrew and archaeology with the Hebrew University in Jerusalem.

Included with his academic studies was being head wrestling coach of college teams.

Dr. Culver has had nineteen years of parish work in the cities of New York and Chicago, and three years of teaching on the seminary level. Pastoral experience includes the ghettos of Harlem. In 1981 he completed a three-year term as an elected member of the Theological Examination Committee for the General Assembly of the Presbyterian Church in America. He served as the President of the National Foundation for the Study of Religion and Economics in Greensboro, North Carolina from 1982 to 1985.

By invitation he attended eight White House Conferences in 1984-85. In April 1986 he was invited by Secretary of State George Schultz to a State Department Conference on South Africa. He has addressed church conferences, university faculties, service clubs, industrial and professional societies, and research associations across the United States, Canada, South America, and the Near East. He speaks and reads Hebrew and German, and reads Latin, Greek, and Akkadian. His authorship includes three books and several hundred published articles.

Dr. Culver is married and the father of six children, one of whom has already graduated into Eternity.

He believes the intelligent giving of self and one's substance is the single greatest source of satisfaction and joy in this life.

ECONOMICS AND POVERTY

Douglas J. Culver

INTRODUCTION

It is a privilege to be here. I have been on the campus a time or two before but informally and to renew a long and deep friendship and affection for Brother Paul Goelz.

I want to turn immediately to my topic by suggesting that I wish to address this in its most rudimentary, bedrock, elemental way.

Sometimes the particularization into almost a fine dust obscures the great overarching principle, which, once grasped, gives us a hold, a purchase, on the magnitude of little irritations and troubles or complexities that cannot be reduced to manageable form if we take them one at a time.

I am suggesting that great ideas are just that kind of thing, and I introduce my remarks with a little story from my own family.

When we lived in Brooklyn, of which you have heard Pastor Neuhaus speak, we lived not far from the same neighborhood where he was, and my four sons were young then. We lived in a neighborhood where two blocks to the west of us was Sacred

Heart Parish, six blocks to the east of us, toward Manhattan, was Saint Patrick's Parish, a very large parish with a fine parochial school. But my sons were the offspring of a Presbyterian minister. They were well instructed in the catechism, but they were not sufficiently well instructed to know that there are other kinds of Christians who go by slightly different labels, though they have many things in common.

On this particular afternoon my second son, named Stewart, came home, and he had an enormous black eye, blood oozing from his mouth, holding his forehead. He had obviously been in a fracas of some kind, and I asked him, "How did it happen? Don't you realize that you are the son of a minister? This just doesn't fly; it doesn't work here."

He said, "Well, I was over at the O'Reilly's," which was two doors down, "making smart remarks about the Pope."

I said, "Son, with a name like O'Reilly and in this neighborhood, did you not realize that they are Catholic?"

He said, "Yea, I knew they were, but I didn't know that the Pope was."

Needless to say, something fundamental was missing from his education, something basic, something so transparently obvious — that was the only reason it had the least bit of humor for you or for me, although it didn't then.

My topic is "Economics and Poverty." I am going to try to resurrect again how very basic that is. Go back with me in the history of man approximately two hundred years. What was the universal condition of all mankind wherever you looked except for a handful of the eugenically born, of the highly born, of the nobility? Poverty. Grinding, monotonous poverty.

POVERTY TWO HUNDRED YEARS AGO

At about the time of the birth of our Nation, the average Frenchman — and they were the better off in continental Europe — spent ninety percent of an entire family's income for bread, bread alone. In Germany, the household of four had about what a thousand dollars would do for four people in the U.S.A. in 1986. Would you like to live on that? In Africa the wheel had not been invented. Medicine everywhere was primarily incantatory, magical. Life was, according to Victor Hugo, base, barren, brutish, and brief.

And one last thing that the same author sought to write about, when he characterized his age, he called it "Les Miserables," the miserables.

I want to repeat: The normal, most elementary rudiment of human experience since time began is "poverty." What changed it? Why do we have so much, why do we have so much to complain about?

Well, about two hundred years ago the principal mind which undergirded the change was Adam Smith, who was not an economist but a moral philosopher, and we need to remember that; before his *Wealth of Nations* he authored *The Theory of Moral Sentiments*, which is the necessary predecessor to it. He saw that a basic moral, spiritual fabric had to be in place and operational before any of the rest of it would work because it was based on a trust system. The harvest was unknown, but the harvest could not possibly be produced in the ancient regime with its merciless restrictions and a monarchy's heavy hand. Freedom to try it depended on, above all, the minds and spirit and inventiveness of a free people. Turn them loose.

Now, I want to add that, in addition to what did come as a turning loose, there was the evangelical preaching of John and Charles Wesley, George Whitefield, and somewhat later from this country Dwight Moody; and there happened in England, from where we have our heritage, something almost unbelievable.

ECONOMIC CHANGE

From the beginning of this period for the next hundred years something happened. The average lifespan at the beginning of that period was, as Michael Novak so happily put it, twenty-nine years for the oppressed sex, twenty-six years for the oppressor sex — there must be something good about oppression. By the time fifty years had passed, lifespans had doubled, and in another fifty years they had gone up another twenty-five or twenty-six years to what they are approximately now. In that period of time the increase of diet, the production of the farmer, the development of the various kinds and breeds of cattle and sheep and poultry simply exploded because those who produced them could now profit from their production. Infant mortality fell from approximately five out of ten – and of that five who survived, two more died before the age of two. By the way, with lifespans of twenty-six and twenty-nine years, when you stood in front of a minister and promised to love, honor, and obey until death do us part, it was no big deal.

Adam Smith accurately saw and prophesied the very thing that we have now seen take place in the radical disparity between what happened in South America and what happened in North America. South America, much more blessed in resources, was simply plundered and its gold and silver carted off some place else, principally Spain and Portugal, where that enormous wealth was dissipated in various ways.

But in this country development began to take place to the extent that over the years at rates of one and two percent there was a growth in what Mr. and Mrs. Average had for disposable goods and services at their command. In the first fifty years it went up a hundred percent, and in that same period of time life spans almost trebled to about seventy years. Population, because the infant mortality rate declined, had an increase that had not happened before, and the population, because of the increase in affluence and diet and so forth, quadrupled to four times more people.

Now, a quick yardstick on that leads me to suggest that there must be a dynamic worth examining when, within the space of one century, which is not that long in human history, a one thousand, six hundred percent betterment in what ordinary people had at their disposal to eat, consume, use, and spend occurred. Think of that. We had better use very great care before we begin to demolish the structure of that society, the institutions which defend and protect it, and the ideals and morality which lie at the base of it.

AN APPROACH TO POVERTY

Something has happened again, and I speak to you now with some prejudice. It is anecdotal, it comes from my personal experience, it comes from my decade spent in the cities of New York and Newark. I do not know where Newark is going, to Heaven or Hell; but wherever it is going, it is going to get there ahead of everybody else. I am the father of a sizeable family and an orthodox, traditional Christian. You will have to keep those all in mind as I recite my own experience in trying to address these very same circumstances in my own life and work.

It was 1966; I was twenty-eight years of age; I was athletic by makeup, rather sunny in disposition, cheerful; I was newly ordained; and I was going to save the world. The great social programs were just beginning to get solidly underway. The years ahead promised great good if they were fully implemented. The brightest and best minds that could be found were in servitude to that great achievement. There were noble intentions. Certain success seemed sure. And money was flowing everywhere and in such amounts that it was slopping over into all kinds of spheres of activity which are not normally influenced by financial or public policy decisions.

I accepted a call to a parish in Brooklyn. It was working class whites, principally southern Europeans. I set out to demonstrate once and forever that courage, timing, and enough hard work and sufficient resources could change maybe not the whole world but certainly my parish. There were distressing conditions right, left, and center. "Surely," I prayed, "please God, these things would yield to the training, knowledge, caring; giving alms, food stamps; the institution of direct concern of all intelligent people – all of whom would receive benefits, including me. In the name of the Father, Amen."

I believed in then, and still do, what is called a holistic

ministry – body, mind, and spirit – the indivisible. The Christian gospel encompasses all of life, and our greater creeds assure us of this. The Apostles' Creed tells us of the resurrection of the body for eternal life, not just the soul. Christian faith, you see, is both incorporeal, invisible and spiritual, as well as corporeal.

With these positive assurances, I was prepared to work until my heart burst, along with many other fine people who were engaged in a search for the grail to cure social ills. If we needed money, we applied for it, and I must say in all fairness, we got most of what we asked for. I interceded with all of these fine folks in officialdom, all the welfare officers, police, juvenile court officers, social workers, teachers, and so on and so on. Most of the time we got what we wanted.

Reflection on this chapter of my life still jars me, though it was experienced more than half a generation ago. I participated so much, I spent myself recklessly and, in fact, wound up in the hospital three times with everything from ulcer problems to heart problems. But the tragic social confrontation – underemployment, unemployment, official corruption, illiteracy, illegitimacy, bastardy – continued ever more rapidly. They did not abate. In fact, there seemed to be a spiral in the fragmentation from what had been a healthy, if also poor, hard-working community.

These problems simply overwhelmed me. They slopped into every corner and cranny of my parish and my personal life. Perhaps you have not tried to calm a crazed twenty-year-old on a jag, a speed trip, crashing into the living room of our apartment above the church at 3:00 o'clock in the morning, or seeking a place to care for a fourteen-year-old girl whose brothers sold her services to support their heroin habits. By the way, I kidnapped that girl and took her out to some friends in New Jersey and put her on a farm. Her father came and was going to kill me, drunk out of his mind, and her brothers were the same. They were six foot seven types. The police told me that if they filed charges, I was dead meat. But I took her anyway. She is now a fine Christian woman, the mother of three, and I hear from her every year at Christmas.

SUBSIDIZING DEPENDENCY AND IRRESPONSIBILITY

To my chagrin and horror, I was finally forced to acknowledge that I had helped set in motion a perfectly rational process, a process which made dependence throughout life not only attractive but possible. I was helping to subsidize irresponsibility.

Can I prove it? No. But I do add that my carefully nourished goals were strikingly similar to the impulses of the aroused Christian conscience which at least echoed in much public policy, as shown in the Bishops' Pastoral Letter on the U.S. Economy; and most of this is debated in our city halls and legislatures.

It is my duty as a faithful shepherd of God's flock to strengthen and help the poor up and out of poverty, up and out of sin. Caring adequately and, if necessary, indefinitely for the truly helpless, the fatherless, the widow, is the Christian's responsibility, period! No ifs, no ands, no buts, no maybes.

The radical investment of time and devotion during that span of years in the sixties and seventies deserved better than it got. That's the rub, you see. How can we make human beings better without making the long-term situation worse? I had made it worse. It was truly an enormous amount of work and an equally impressive investment in time and emotion.

It is true there is entirely too much evil in this world: hunger, and cold, and disease, and fear and hate, and wrenching, and self-seeking wiles of the mindless. But may I add: Thank God, indeed we do live in a spiritual universe. If we leave that unaddressed, we lose everything else.

It is right to address the needs of the poor. For that reason, I suggest I have a moral and Christian responsibility to use every method at my command that those who represent me in matters of public policy so structure and protect me and our institutions, so that the mandated agencies of society guarantee option and openness.

I want to help the poor along, but for the last two generations and a half, command economies with their central control have fallen short, terribly short. It is as if the same terrible hand that wrote on the hall of Belshassar's palace has now written on our ideas as well, "Weighed and found wanting."

You see, the premises of our position were wrong. We were touting excellence, self-discipline, success, and prosperity; and we were rewarding failure, lack of self-discipline, immorality, and non-work. Let me ask you – judge for yourselves – why should you be surprised that you got less success, more irresponsibility, less self-sufficiency? You see, a dangerous consensus had been proclaimed, albeit however heartfelt the desire was to help. The recipients were frightfully crippled.

A REAPPRAISAL

The City of New York, which I love, serves nicely as an acronym for the best and worst of these elements. The tragedy of that city is that we cannot acknowledge the wreckage brought on by half a century of corrupt public policy. The ruin is magnificent, to be sure, but it is a ruin. If anybody knows the reasons for this kind of calamity, really Christians should. Genuineness, value, and use are spiritual qualities bound inextricably to a Biblical view of civilization – man made in the image of God. Our internal lives always come into the external and shape the world beneath His hand. To change only the exterior is not only to hold up a cruel fiction but to be idolators. It is to drape the Messianic mantle over hopeless expectations. There is nothing more worthless.

Along with these presuppositions which I presume,let me ask you, with some sense of trembling, to reconsider some basic elements again as we address the truth in our own late Twentieth Century.

Let us look again at what Saint Paul, Augustine, the Greek Councils, my own Reformation heritage teach about the foibles of mankind. If bureaucrats suddenly partake only of purity, what will you have while all others are tinctured by sin? Life on this earth will always be marked by struggles with faith and true humility for our fears. There will be alienation and physical death. We are to strive against these calamities but it will be uphill against the flesh every inch. We are doing it in obedience to Christ. We will win some battles, lose many, and the final victory will be Christ's alone, as is promised, at the Second Advent.

But short of this ultimate equitable state of affairs which only He can bring, what means are available to us to redistribute wealth without destroying incentives to produce it in the first place? To whom shall we appeal to make the decisions about what constitutes equity? Where will we find the minds to administer this tremendous apparatus? And how will we pay for it once it is in place?

Let me add here as a footnote. I think I am correct in this, if we took just the money for those designated as those below that magical poverty line and divided it up, hypothetically; supposing that everybody who is constituted in a four-member family or just four people and gave them their portion of that money, do you know what the division would be? My figures are about $42,000 per four-member family.

Where, therefore, does all that money go? Inside the green belt of Washington, D.C. is where seventy-five percent of it goes. Who has a vested interest in the poverty business? I will leave that to your own deductions.

THE DISCIPLINE OF THE FAMILY

The worth and dignity of every person encompasses such virtues, among others, as charity, restraint of passion, and so forth; I know something about that. How do you imagine that a man like me has dealt with four young men, his sons, all of whom are bigger and stronger, faster, smarter, and better-looking that he is, in the "Playboy" epoch? What in the world do you think I did to restrain them? I'll tell you what I did. It started when they were three and four and five and six. I paddled the daylights out of them when they broke the rules. The only Department of Health, Education and Welfare that will ever work is the family, the monogamous, traditional family. Do not ever let anybody con you about anything else. It simply ain't so. And you are talking to a man who spent most of his adult life working in the very vortex of every liberal and progressive idea that has been, and that is the City of New York. It didn't work.

When Christian pulpits, pastors, priests, the agencies, the institutions of those churches, and all manner of ecclesiastical managers and officers turn to non-religious preoccupations, whom are we to go to for responsible action when righteousness languishes?

I will not soon forget as part of my experience, my embarrassed chagrin, I guess I wasn't embarrassed for I expected it, when I expounded in 1966 the notion that chastity was not only the best way to prevent pregnancy among teenage girls but a host of other maladies that go with it; that it not only was a crime against God but it was a crime against reason and sanity to think and speak otherwise — I didn't win many disciples.

THE FAILURE OF THE CHURCHES

What has happened to the converting, civilizing, and creative morality that has been endemic to Christianity? They have now become low-priority matters but rarely experienced, even while the social program expands and parish participation moves toward soap opera banality. The spiritually hungry are not hungry anymore — they are starved. Traditional, Biblical persuasive preaching and consistent ministry are in desperately short supply. A famine is in progress.

On the other hand, Protestant commercialism, and by that I mean taxing and spending, cannot effectively replace the binding effect of our societal structure, the family circle. Please do not confuse the word "society" with the word "government." They are not the same.

I do not expect every person to put on a robe or be a believer in Christ, whether he is a Roman Catholic, a Presbyterian, as I am, a Baptist, or independent. The qualities of moral persuasion and generous impulses which encourage giving that checks but does not restrain evil are attributes over which we need not be powerless. We must stop apologizing for the fundamental correlation between religious faith and the maintenance of a vital political autonomy. I will remind you that it was the Father of our Country who taught us that the first political institution is the Christian religion, and for Washington it was the religious creeds, in his case the thirteen Articles of the Church of England.

THE CONSEQUENCES

For most of us, though not for all by any means, the doctrine of accountability to our Heavenly Father on a daily basis in everything we do is a marvelous carrot-and-stick, promoting all kinds of productive activity. Illicit sex, drugs, rejection of religious values along the highway of life, departure from strictly traditional forces, have helped make suicide into a major killer of young people.

I wish you could go with me just once and pick up an emaciated, sore, oozing flesh of a young girl whom I remember, put her in a box in the ground; or cut one down from the rafters, and do it time after time and try to say something consoling to the parents or loved ones. I am not saying these things simply out of bookish learning. I was there in the stench of death for a long, long time. It broke me on the wheel.

It is worse; it is not better. What will prophets say if we fail in these matters? Certainly the adults who avow the principles that they have now must be more consistent. We not only must pronounce the Ten Commandments; you and I must obey them; and we must stop exploiting and congratulating public figures, and celebrating and paying out enormous funds to those who flaunt them, for whatever reason, be it entertainment or otherwise.

The only thing it seems we are able to do is to agitate for more or fuller employment, better or more daycare centers, better and longer education, a stronger economy. Will all of these help us? Frankly, I doubt it. For I think we have gotten the equation on backwards. Curiously enough, the old Christian virtues were productive of that for which we are striving.

Think, for example, to use just one small illustration, what a blow might be dealt poverty, the major portion of which continues to exist in households headed by single females, if males did not abandon their duty to their families. If the facts are correct, and mine are from the *U. S. News and World Report*, a series of articles in late 1984, unwed mothers and broken marriages account for the single largest category of persons under the poverty line, more than all other categories cumulatively. It is a moral, spiritual problem, not merely an economic one or a political one.

Let me be more blunt. The greatest society in the world, is the War on Poverty, by whatever other labels we have called such exertions: a trillion dollars spent, more or less, with fine intentions, the best minds, armed with computers, have actually led on to worsened conditions – generated dependence, accelerated disintegration of poor families, increased educational failure.

Just this week the long study on our four-year colleges came out. The bottom line is they stink. There are a few exceptions, I am happy to report, that are among the church-affiliated, smaller, independent colleges like this one. In fact, one writer says most graduates do not have what high school graduates had two generations ago. Now, if you have paid the tuition bills that I have paid in the last eighteen years, that makes you angry. These colleges have steadily pushed greater numbers into the ranks of the poor, people who have been professionally targeted for help. The consequence makes sheer common sense. The cause is a concept of self-sufficiency that has systematically and oppressively destroyed initiative in individuals in favor of society as a whole, both philosophically and in what some people like to call practicality. Standing on one's achievements or accomplishments is no longer held in regard in a welfare state society, and this has become the chief wisdom. It is palpable nonsense.

So what is it about us who realize the necessity of a spiritual ingredient that calls for action among our poverty folk? Recognition of the problems can grow cold. The enormous exertions of the past two generations and a half have not succeeded but have aggravated the situation. The spiritual accountability has not been fulfilled; indeed, it is past due. We are not to stop trying to help the poor, but we cannot take into account only the material realities.

NOT BY BREAD ALONE

I am reminded of the words of Saint Paul, that this present world is a shadow of reality. Economic cures by themselves are not cures. Our Lord and Savior appealed closer to the truth when he called us to the true reality. He said, "Man does not live by bread alone but by every word that proceeds from the mouth of God."

May I add: I think this is true even when every loaf of bread is guaranteed by a seemingly omnipotent state. It is true in this cold, broken, ponderous, sick, dark, sin-ridden world that we have an obligation to produce, and to give, and to help, and to reassure, and comfort all we can, everywhere we can. It is also clear that we are not to make dependency possible.

A spiritual renaissance, Lord, starting with me.

I thank you.

Discussion

Question: You speak very well to the moral issues of poverty and what to do with poverty in general terms, but some of the poverty in the United States is in ghetto areas. I am wondering if you might contrast that kind of poverty with the kind of poverty you have in the Third World countries, Central and South America?

Douglas Culver:

I have not traveled all that much, though I have been to Central and South America a time or two. My guess is that of the help available in so-called central city or ghetto areas, it is greater than anything the Third World dreams of, although I can't substantiate that. In North Africa, where I have been, the Far East, and certain sections of cities that I have visited in Venezuela and Colombia and in northeastern Brazil, which latter has experienced great crop difficulty, those regions are far worse off than our ghettos economically in terms of the material goods and services that are available.

In our central cities, and this is just an observation, and I am not even sure I should mention it, the principal obstacles are cultural. They are not exclusively the lack of work or unavailability of education or training or anything else of that nature. They are cultural and subcultural problems that are deeply bred into the psyche and the makeup. How to intercept that is a difficult subject.

I personally am a part of two agencies that work in and around the south Bronx, east Harlem, portions of Brooklyn, in fact one of them that Pastor Neuhaus referred to, and West Paterson in New Jersey, where we have adopted a program combining literacy and what we call low-tech schooling. We take the kids that have been so bad that they can't tolerate them in any school, they have been in and out of court and jail. We try to get across the elements of arithmetic enough to add up a column of numbers and to write a check—that kind of rudimentary material—basic literacy to read and hopefully to write, though we don't always succeed with that, and some low-tech training.

We have one fellow who has succeeded as a garbage can maker in Harlem, and in Harlem that is a very important trade. He has a sheet metal machine in his garage, and he makes about $40,000 a year; he has hired the second man on the strength of the $40,000. He has also married a woman who had six children and has taken them off the welfare role, so he is a benefit to the larger body as well.

But we have emphasized not recreation, not fun and games, but basic literacy and a trade, and also some Christian training is involved. We are succeeding modestly with that. But we do not supply any money or give any money. It is not a remunerative or welfare proposition at all. You have to come and sweat.

Comment:

It sounds something similar to the Peace Corps' original function.

Douglas Culver:

Yes, and we have a couple of ex-marines running it for us. We have found that lesser types just cannot handle them.

Erik von Kuehnelt-Leddihn:

Although I agree with your general premise, my observation is that poverty in America bites much more.

Douglas Culver:

That is a good way to put it.

Erik von Kuehnelt-Leddihn:

In other words, the poor American suffers more in his ego, in his dignity, his personality. Now, for instance, there are terrible slums in Italy, but there is no skid row, which is something else. A man does not exist alone in poverty there; there are family ties that come from all sides. There are no real slums in Austria, no slums in Germany, no slums in Belgium. In other words, there is a whole area that is poor. There is a surprising percentage of Americans, and I can only use the word, you are improvident; in other words, you are not really future-minded, you look only to the day at hand, and then suddenly something has caused an emergency vis-a-vis being prepared for something less.

I think here, for instance, of the collapse of *Collier's Magazine* now fifteen years ago, when about ten days before Christmas, all its employees were sent a wire on Saturday, "Don't come to *Collier's* on Monday. It exists no longer."

That is an experience I had, which I have lived through, not that I was employed by *Collier's*, but I had a letter of recommendation and rang up after the announcement and a voice replied to my call for an appointment, "Have you seen today's newspaper?"

JOHN CARDINAL KROL

JOHN CARDINAL KROL

John Cardinal Krol was ordained on February 20, 1937. He was appointed Titular Bishop of Cadi and Auxiliary Bishop of Cleveland on July 11, 1953 and consecrated on September 2, 1953. He was promoted to Archbishop of Philadelphia on February 11, 1961 and created Cardinal Priest on June 26, 1967. He is spiritual leader to 1.3 million Catholics in the Philadelphia Archdiocese. On February 20, 1987 he celebrated his Fiftieth year as a priest; some 2,000 people attended the Mass, breaking into applause as Krol, wearing garments of scarlet, gold, and white lace, left the flower-filled altar.

Cardinal Krol has served under seven Popes and participated in the Second Vatican Council. His is a Papal Appointee to the 15-member Prefecture of Economic Affairs of the Holy See. He has been chosen as the Pro-President of "The Extraordinary Synod of Bishops" held recently in Rome.

As one of the first Presidents of the National Council of Catholic Bishops, Cardinal Krol is recognized as one of the most influential leaders of the Catholic Church, both on the national and international levels.

He serves on President Reagan's "Advisory Committee for the Private Sector Initiatives."

A long litany of citations and honors graciously accepted in the name of Him whom he serves, offers evidence in abundance of

Cardinal Krol's achievements: he has received more than a score of Honorary Doctorates from universities across the nation; he has been honored for his public leadership in confronting and exposing the evils of secular humanism; and has been cited for his outstanding leadership in combating the social evils of our day.

In recognition of his achievements and inspirational leadership in the Church, the William Joseph Chaminade Award for Distinguished Spiritual Leadership was bestowed upon his Eminence, John Cardinal Krol, Archbishop of Philadelphia, by St. Mary's University. This Award is named for the Founder of the Marianist Order which operates St. Mary's University. It is conferred on contemporary leaders who devote their lives to social progress throughout the world.

MORAL WISDOM IN THE
ALLOCATION
OF ECONOMIC RESOURCES

John Cardinal Krol

INTRODUCTION

In his formal invitation, relative to my participation in this extraordinary Symposium, your President, Rev. John A. Leies, identified the direction to be taken in this Symposium when he said that "your School of Business and Administration is committed to formulating and articulating the values of the Judeo-Christian tradition and the philosophical concepts of the United States Constitution as they inform the Market System of the American Economy."

The presentations which you have already heard have, for the most part, adopted the practical approach. "Economics in Catholic Countries"; "Ethics and Economics"; and, "Economics and Poverty," attest to this. My own presentation, one that is identified with the title of the Symposium itself, must therefore re-establish the principles which have prevailed and must continue to prevail, wherever the "allocation of human resources" is discussed.

Acccordingly, in formulating this address, I have divided it into three parts. In the First I shall attempt to place the Symposium itself within the universal environment of the traditional and philosophical concepts that have been mentioned above. This must be done in order to identify the values that inspired our Nation's Founders – especially with regard to the systems that were chosen by our forefathers to contribute to the fulfillment of the Freedom which was won by them. In Part Two, I shall review the principles that must be identified and categorically applied to all economic systems, including our own. This will offer the opportunity to point out the differences in the acceptance and application of these principles, as they have been variously accepted and practiced in other parts of the world. And, in Part Three, I shall permit the Church to speak for itself with regard to all these points. This will be done by citing certain pronouncements and promulgations which have identified and applied the major principles that must direct the ongoing actions of those whose authority demands a responsibility that must match that authority.

PHILOSOPHICAL CONCEPTS OF THE MARKET SYSTEM

Nineteen Hundred and Eighty-Six marked the celebration of two anniversaries which were related to the topic which we are to discuss tonight: both the Texas Sesquicentennial and the One Hundredth Anniversary of the Statue of Liberty identify the centerpiece of Liberty and Freedom upon which our Nation is founded. This year, we add a third celebration: the 200th Anniversary of the United States Constitution.

To recall these anniversaries, and to identify their profound significance, offers us an opportunity to place ourselves in the position of the Founders of our Nation, not only to reflect on the Victory for Freedom itself, but also, to learn from them the method that was used to carry forward the process of implementation—a process which was as difficult as the achievement of the initial victory itself; and, a process which continues in its difficulty to this day, both on the national and on the local level, where we are gathered here to discuss "Moral Wisdom in the Allocation of Human Resources."

In order to learn from the Founders of our Nation, therefore, we have to transfer ourselves to a meeting that must have taken place after the achievement of Victory and Freedom.

As they gathered to celebrate their newly won Freedom, two extremely difficult problems had to be faced and resolved. Phrased in the form of questions, the leaders had to answer, first, "Now that we have won our freedom, how do we implement it on the personal, the social, the political, and the religious levels?"; and, as a derivative of the first, "What kind of systems must we design to implement this Freedom, on each of these levels?"

History shows that the Nation's leaders confronted and met these challenges in a way that still stands as an example for the rest of the world to follow. We know that their choice of a political democracy, built upon a reverence for the dignity of the person and upon the inalienable rights with which the Creator endowed that person, brought with it a Constitution that embodied that dignity and those rights.

We know, too, that when the choice of an economic system had to be made, that choice was based on the inherent characteristics of that "dignity." That demanded the right to own private property—always coupled with its correlative responsibility for the proper use of that property and its relationship to the common good of all; the right to choose one's vocation and the locale of that vocation; and, the right to exercise responsibly one's own free initiative in the entrepreneurial realm. All of these are to be accompanied by, and dependent on, a knowledge and practice of a responsibility to the Common Good of all.

Faced with these rights—and with their counterparts, the duties that accompanied them—our Forefathers freely accepted the only correct choice: a free economic system that fostered the democratic principles that undergird each and every one of these rights and duties. In effect, they opted for a philosophy of Free Enterprise which they understood and intended to practice as an "Enterprise in Freedom Itself." This philosophy would make it mandatory to make the decisions that would have to be made with regard to the proper allocation of human resources. A system would have to be created that would emphasize not only the dignity attached to "work," but also, and most significantly, to the "justice" that was itself essentially related to the dignity of the person; to his inalienable rights; and, to the Source of that dignity, namely, the Creator Himself.

We have, thus far, identified, first, a commitment to articulating the values of the Judeo-Christian tradition and the philosophical concepts of the United States Constitution; second, the choice of systems made by the Founders of our Nation; and, third, the centrality of the Symposium in which we are now participating. It must already have become obvious that one principle joins all these inextricably together. Simply stated, that principle declares that all systems, whether they be political, social, or economic, are predetermined to carry forward, to develop, and to fulfill, the underlying "philosophy of the person" held by their designers—a philosophy of the person in whose image and likeness all systems are to be selected.

An essential derivative of this principle relates it inextricably to our immediate project: the allocation of human resources will always follow the moral wisdom attached to the philosophy of the person that undergirds any particular system that is designed to carry out this philosophy.

Analysts and other professional students of "systems" have not always identified, emphasized, and applied this principle. If it were to be applied, it would lend credence to the "correct effort" to compare and evaluate different systems, from the point of view of their underlying philosophies, rather than from the point of view that merely compares the constituents of the system without referring these constituents to the philosophies which have predetermined them.

Can we test this critical evaluation? To do so, we must ourselves identify and analyze the method which has been "traditionally used," relative to the differentiation between economic systems themselves.

PRINCIPLES FOR EVALUATING ECONOMIC SYSTEMS

Economists have traditionally defined their own area of concern in terms of the relationship between the finite goods available to all and the infinite demands made upon that finite inventory. Accordingly, production, distribution, and consumption, have found their own definitive identification and practice in terms of this relationship and the resolutions that have been offered to it. Implied, but rarely identified and emphasized, is the fact that the resolutions that have been offered by a variety of different "systems" depend, essentially and incontrovertibly, on the conception of the person held by each—a conception in terms of which, whether admitted or not, the selections have themselves been made.

Specifically, the question of the allocation of human resources cannot be properly discussed, unless and until, the conceptions of the human person held by those who recommend different allocations, are contrasted and dissectingly compared. In other words, the conceptions held by different designers of systems with regard to the ownership of property; with regard to the ownership of the means of production; with regard to the relationship of labor and capital, vis-a-vis, the human person and his rights; etc.; cannot be critically evaluated, unless and until, the underlying conception of the person, in terms of which the choices have been made, are themselves identified and evaluated. In effect, "systems," standing apart from the conception of the person in whose image they were designed, cannot be properly compared and evaluated. To attempt to do so, is to leave out of consideration the major determining factor that actually dictated the choices concerning ownership, production, distribution, etc., in the first place. In fine, no conclusion with regard to the proper allocation of human resources can legitimately be made without first identifying the underlying conception of the person that dictated that conclusion.

Thus, it must become obvious to all that any determination with regard to the proper allocation of human resources must recognize that they are intimately related to the ownership of private property and to the ownership of the means of production. One cannot compare a system based on the conception of the person endowed by the Creator with inalienable rights to a system based on the conception of the person identified as a chattel of an all powerful state from whence his "rights" emanate. There can be no evaluation of one system that accepts the ownership of private property as a right of the person with one that denies this right to the person. The latter system places the means of production in the hands of the state and the other places them in the hands of individual persons. These two cannot be equated.

We have seen, from what has been said, that the Founding Fathers based their selection of all systems, including the economic systems—together with its resulting determinations with regard to the proper allocations of human resources—on a conception of the person that identified his inherent dignity and the basic rights that accompanied that dignity. And, we have seen by inference, that those who embrace another system, commonly called Marxist "socialism," have chosen that system precisely because their determinations with regard to the allocation of human resources depend on a conception of the person that stresses his dependent relationship to the state, with the inevitable result that the interpretations that are offered to the ownership of property and the ownership of the means of production, are themselves predetermined by a conception of the person that undergirds the Marxist socialistic system itself.

Where, then, does the Church itself stand?

To secure the proper response to this question—and also, to point out the proximity of that response, or the aversion of that response, to any other particular system and its determinations with regard to the allocation of human resources – is to follow the teachings of the Church with regard to the dignity of the person, especially as these are related to human rights and to the inviolate dictates of these rights. That is, with regard to the ownership of private property; with regard to the ownership of the means of production; with regard to the manner assigned to the distribution and consumption of goods; and, with regard to the justice that must be exercised in the proper allocation of all human resources – recourse must be made to values, concepts, and principles.

It is now the turn of the Church to speak out on all of these matters.

THE CHURCH SPEAKS

Time and again, the Church has emphasized the right to life, liberty, and the pursuit of happiness, as well as the derivatives of these rights. This emphasis is found in pre-and post-Vatican II as well as in conciliar documents. I cite one such document, which is not well-known and rarely cited. It was my privilege to read this document at the 1974 Synod of Bishops in Rome. This statement, approved by the Synod Fathers, was issued by Pope Paul VI as the message from the Synod.

I cite a part of the Introduction of the message: "Human dignity is rooted in the image and reflection of God in each of us. It is this which makes all persons essentially equal. The integral development of persons makes more clear the Divine Image in them. In our time the Church has grown more deeply aware of this truth. Hence, she believes firmly that the promotion of human rights is required by the Gospel and is central to her ministry."

The message calls attention to certain rights most threatened today.

I. The right to life. This right is basic and inalienable. It is grievously violated by abortion and euthanasia, by wide-spread torture, by acts of violence against innocent parties, and by the scourge of war.

II. The right to eat. This right is directly linked to the right to life. Millions today face starvation.

III. Socio-economic rights. Massive disparities of power and wealth in the world, often within nations, concentration of economic power in the hands of a few nations and multi-national groups, structural imbalances, unemployment, and discriminatory employment practices, all require reform.

IV. Politico-cultural rights. People should have the right to shape their own destinies; to participate freely and responsibly in the political process; free access to information; freedom of speech and the press, as well as freedom of dissent. They have a right to be educated and to determine the education of their children. They must be secure from arrest, torture, and imprisonment for political or ideological reasons, and all must be guaranteed juridical protection of their personal, social, cultural, and political rights.

V. The right of religious liberty. This right uniquely reflects the dignity of the person as this is known from the word of God and from reason itself. All must acknowledge the right of religious liberty in words and foster it in deeds and eliminate any type of discrimination.

This brief message of the Bishops' Synod of 1974 illustrates the Church's teaching and concern about all human rights. With reference to the allocation of human resources, other derivative rights should be mentioned, namely:

1) The right to work and to the means of dignified subsistence;

2) The right to the respect for the person's bodily integrity; to the respect for personal property; and to the respect for the person's carefully won reputation;

3) The right to his material and spiritual development, which may be sought through the right to free participation in associations;

4) The right to the acquisition of the just means necessary for the attainment of personal dignity: namely, that dignity which reflects the image of God which is impressed upon each person.

These developmental rights, together with all the other derivatives that find their own existence in the exercise of these rights, find their true origin in the Creator Himself; and, they therefore bring with them, the correlative duties to direct their exercise towards the person's ultimate destiny as this is inextricably related to the Creator.

> Any human society, if it is to be well ordered and productive, must lay down, as a foundation, this principle: namely, that every human being is a person, that is, his nature is endowed with intelligence and free will. Indeed, precisely because he is a person he has rights and obligations flowing directly and simultaneously from his own nature. And as the rights and obligations are universal and inviolable, they cannot in any way be surrendered.
>
> *Pacem in Terris*, John XXIII, 9, 10.

There is a growing awareness of the exalted dignity proper to the human person, since he stands above all things and his rights and duties are universal and inviolable.

Gaudium et Spes, the Pastoral Constitution on the Church in the Modern World, Vatican II, 26, states:

> Every man has a right to life, to bodily integrity, and to the means which are suitable for the proper development of life; these are primarily food, clothing, shelter, rest, medical care, and finally, the necessary social services. Therefore, a human being also has the right to security in cases of sickness, inability to work, unemployment, or in any case in which he is deprived of the means of subsistence through no fault of his own.

Pacem in Terris, John XXIII, 11, also states:

> Human beings have the right to choose freely the state of life which they prefer and, therefore, the right to set up a family with equal rights and duties for man and

woman, and also the right to follow a vocation to the priesthood or the religious life.

We see evidence here in abundance of the tremendous balance between those rights which manifest the greatness of the Free Enterprise philosophy of the person and those rights that manifest the correlative responsibilities that accrue to the possession and exercise of these rights.

Speaking specifically to economic rights, we hear the Church echo Pius XI, Leo XIII, and Pius XII, when it says, with regard to work, wages, and distributive justice – carefully balanced against property rights:

> Man has the right by the natural law not only to an opportunity to work, but also, to go about his work without coercion.... The worker has the right to a wage determined according to the criterion of justice, and sufficient therefore, in proportion to the available resources (sic), to give the worker and his family a standard of living in keeping with the dignity of the human person.

As in all other cases, the Church never veers from the principle, that it is the dignity of the person that should dictate the allocation of human resources. In this connection, the Church has always and steadfastly championed the right to the ownership of private property, coupled always with the responsibility that accompanies the right to ownership as this is related to the common good of all.

Thus:

> The right to private property, even of productive goods, also derives from the nature of man.... This right is an effective means for safeguarding the dignity of the human person and for the exercise of responsibility in all fields; it strengthens and frees serenity to family life, thereby increasing the peace and prosperity of the State.

> However, it is opportune to point out that there is a

social duty essentially inherent in the right of private property.

Pacem in Terris, John XXIII, 18-22.

At this point, we have to emphatically affirm that our own responsibility to achieve a proper balance in our portrayal of the Church's position on the "right to own private property," requires that we stress the following principles. This is especially needed because of the recurrence of certain false interpretations becoming rampant in our day—false interpretations which confuse the priorities offered to the ownership of private property by the Church.

Therefore, we must always stress:

1) that a person deserves to possess the fruits of his labor in some significant form;
2) that material goods are absolutely necessary for the maintenance of human life;
3) that experience shows that the possession of goods is a safeguard to liberty;
4) and, that the right to ownership includes the right to the free and reasonable use of these goods.

In this connection, too, it is commandingly necessary to distinguish between the Church's critical evaluation of negative or pejorative "capitalism" and "Free Enterprise Capitalism." It must, in effect, be made crystal clear that the Church has never considered the capitalistic system to be inherently evil, whereas it has always unswervingly declared the Marxist socialistic system to be intrinsically evil.

Leo XIII's whole effort, Pius XI has warned us, was to adjust the economic regime (capitalism) to the standards of true order:

Whence it follows that the system itself (capitalism) is not to be condemned.

Quadragesimo Anno, Pius XI, 101.

All those who today seek to confuse the distinction between

pejorative capitalism and responsible practiced "Free Enterprise Capitalism," must answer to the admonition that it (the capitalistic system) is not vicious of its very nature:

> But it violates right order whenever capital so employs the working or wage earner classes as to direct business and economic activity entirely to its own arbitrary will and advantages, without regard for the human dignity of the workers, the social characteristics of economic life, social justice, and the common good.
> *Quadragesimo Anno*, Pius XI, 101.

To fully understand and to fully grasp the implications of a confusion between pejorative capitalism and Free Enterprise Capitalism; and, to fully comprehend the real attack of the Church on Marxist socialism, which, contrary to its position on Free Enterprise Capitalism, it does consider (Marxist socialism) intrinsically evil, we have to return again and again to Pius XI:

> Whether socialism is considered as a doctrine, or as an historical fact, or as a movement, if it really remains socialism, it cannot be brought into harmony with the dogmas of the Church, even after it has yielded to the truth and justice in the points we have mentioned – the reason being that it conceives human society in a way utterly alien to Christian truth.
> *Quadragesimo Anno*, Pius XI, 114-115, 117.

LIBERATION THEOLOGY

Our admonitions with regard to the errors perpetrated in the treatment of the right to the ownership of private property and its correlative limitations, bring with them the necessity to warn against the excesses of liberation theology. This is especially true where these flagrant excesses – actually paraphrasing the Marxist declarations of the Manifesto of the Communist Party in its opening paragraph – make all values: intellectual, spiritual, economic, political, and social, to be completely dependent on the prevailing forces of production and exchange. These declarations invert the true order of reality, where the Source of all true values – transcendental in their origin and application – is the Creator Himself. Based on this error of liberation theology, it is, therefore, falsely claimed that a change in the prevailing economic system, especially with regard to the allocation of human resources, will automatically change the values upon which the allocation rests. The truth is the other way around: every system, as we have shown previously, is itself completely determined in its content and direction, by the philosophy of life that designed it in the first place.

The Church has already warned us concerning the false inroads of a liberation theology which is all too frequently based on Marxist principles. It is necessary to alert all to the warnings.

CONCLUSION

We have cited only a few ideas of the tremendous inventory from which we could choose in order to demonstrate the Church's continuing emphasis on the principles that are to be meticulously applied whenever the allocation of human resources is the subject of discussion. Merely to open the pages of *Gaudium et Spes* (On the Church in the Modern World); of *Inscrutabili* (On the Evils of Society); of *Libertas Humana* (On Human Liberty); of *Mater et Magistra* (On Christianity and Social Progress); of Populorum Progressio (On the Development of Peoples); of *Quadragesimo Anno* (On Social Reconstruction); of *Quod Apostolici Muneris* (On the Socialists); and of *Rerum Novarum* (On the Condition of the Working Class) is to be confronted with an overwhelming wealth of information on the subject of the proper allocation of human resources.

In this connection, therefore, it is only proper to add, finally, the words of the present Pope, who only recently referred to the thought of his own encyclical, *Laborem Exercens*, when he addressed the residents of barrios in Colombia:

The Creator has been pleased to endow this land of yours with immense resources. On you, accordingly, lies the heavy responsibility to make them bear fruit, so that they may serve the well-being of all. No one may forget that the goods entrusted to man have a universal destiny. . . . For this reason, those who have the responsibility of administering the goods of creation must bear in mind—in conformity with the Divine will—not only their own needs, but also those of all the others, in such a way that no one—but especially the poorest—may remain shut out from access to these goods.

RECOGNITIONS

The Advisory Council
of the
School of Business and Administration
St. Mary's University

JAMES W. ALLEN
Chairman of the Board
San Pedro Bancshares

MICHAEL D. BELDON
President
Beldon Roofing & Remodeling

SAM P. BELL
Partner-in-Charge
Ernst & Whinney

THOMAS BERG
Vice President and Director
Ellison Industries, Inc.

DR. JOHN G. CULL
Clinical Psychologist
Behavioral Medicine Associates, P.A.

DAVID DAVISS
Executive Vice President and COO
La Quinta Motor Inns

GERALD DUBINSKI, SR.
President
Standard Industries

DENNIS F. JUREN
President
Tesoro Petroleum Corporation

STEPHEN M. DUFILHO
Managing Partner
The Quincy Lee Companies

RAY ELLISON
Chairman of the Board
Ellison Industries, Inc.

EDWARD P. GISTARO
President and CEO
Datapoint Corporation

DON HARRELL
President
D. B. Harrell Company

WILLIAM E. HARRELL
Chairman of the Board and CEO
Texas American Bank Fondren
Houston, Texas

A. ROANE HARWOOD
Real Estate Investments

JOHN HOELSCHER
Senior Vice President – Finance
Valero Energy Corporation

LOUIS H. PITLUK
President
The Pitluk Group

PATRICK J. KENNEDY, SR.
Attorney-at-Law

DAVID C. KOCUREK
Registered Representative
Rauscher Pierce Refsnes, Inc.

JANE H. MACON
Partner
Fulbright & Jaworski

DAN F. PARMAN
Chairman of the Board
Parman Interests, Inc.

PAUL REDDY
Managing Partner
Peat Marwick Main & Co.

STANLEY D. ROSENBERG
Oppenheimer, Rosenberg,
Kelleher & Wheatley, Inc.

ALAN L. STINSON
Partner-in-Charge
Deloitte, Haskins & Sells

PAUL J. VAN TUYL
Vice President – Human Resources
USAA Federal Savings Bank

TABLE SPONSORS
for the
Dinner Honoring
JOHN CARDINAL KROL

Angelo Drossos

Barshop Enterprises

Tom Benson

Edward V. Cheviot

Columbia Industries

Ellison Industries

Ernst & Whinney

David C. Kocurek

Peat Marwick Main & Co.

Quincy Lee Interests

Schott, Bartoskewitz & Co.

Tesoro Petroleum Corporation

USAA

Valero Energy Corporation

Victoria Savings Association

We wish to express our deep appreciation to all the
Table Sponsors who are listed, and also to those
whose names we received after press time.

About the Editor

Paul C. Goelz, S.M. is a member of the Society of Mary (Marianists), a Catholic religious Order of Priests and Brothers who conduct schools and universities throughout the world.

He is the Director of the Algur H. Meadows Center for Entrepreneurial Studies at St. Mary's University. Previously he established the Myra Stafford Pryor Chair of Free Enterprise. He was the Dean of the School of Business and Administration from 1962 to 1977.

He earned a Bachelor's degree in Business Administration and a Master of Arts degree from the University of Dayton, and a Master of Business Administration and a Doctor of Philosophy from Northwestern University.

He is the author of articles, books, and research monographs on: industry structures, administrative policy, budgetary control, marketing management, public housing, and higher education.

His experience in business has been in banking, shoe, oil equipment, and automotive industries. Before entering the educational profession he was associated with the International Shoe Company and General Motors Corporation.

A principal academic interest is conducting seminars and institutes for teachers of Free Enterprise.

In addition to his university duties Dr. Goelz serves as a consultant to corporations and government agencies and is on the boards of regional and national associations. He has addressed executive development programs of the U. S. Department of Defense, the U. S. Agency for International Development in Mexico, and professional associations.

He is a member of the Academy of Management, the American Marketing Association, the American Institute of Industrial Engineers, the National Association of Business Economists; is a member of the Board of Directors of Junior Achievement of South Texas, and is an Advisory Trustee of the National Foundation for the Study of Religion and Economics.

For ten years he was a member of the Board of Directors of the American Assembly of Collegiate Schools of Business. He was President of the Southwestern Business Administration Association and for twelve years was a member of the Executive Committee.

He is a co-founder of the Association of Private Enterprise Education and former President of the Association.

He is the Editor of the *Entrepreneurial Commentary*, a publication devoted to economic thought and innnovation.

Dr. Goelz is a Founder and Chairman of the FORUM ON ENTREPREURSHIP. He is listed in Who's Who in America, the Blue Book: Leaders of the English-Speaking World, American Men of Science, and Who's Who in American Education.

In February, 1979 the Freedoms Foundation at Valley Forge conferred on Dr. Goelz the Award for Excellence in Private Enterprise Education. In May, 1982 the San Antonio Young Lawyers Association conferred on him The Liberty Bell Award in public recognition of outstanding community service in the fields of education, business, religion, and youth organizations.

The philosophical and theological interests of Professor Goelz focus on the Freedom of the Individual in the pursuit of economic objectives.